A BREED APART

John Barsness

Thomas BeVier

Paul Carson

Chris Dorsey

Jim Fergus

Gene Hill

John Holt

Michael McIntosh

Dave Meisner

Datus Proper

Jerome Robinson

Diane Vasey

Stuart Williams

A BREED APART

A Tribute to the Hunting Dogs that Own Our Souls

An Original Anthology – Volume II
Edited by Doug Truax

COUNTRYSPORT PRESS
New Albany, Ohio

©1994 by Countrysport, Inc.
Illustrations ©1994 by Bruce Langton

First Edition
10 9 8 7 6 5 4 3 2 1

Published by Countrysport Press
15 South High Street, P.O. Box 166, New Albany, Ohio 43054-0166

Printed in the United States of America

ISBN 0-924357-39-8 Trade Edition
ISBN 0-924357-41-X Deluxe Limited Edition

CONTENTS

INTRODUCTION

by Datus Proper

All of us are hunting for something. We have been after it for at least thirty thousand years, judging from evidence that one of us painted on the walls of a cave, and our search shows no signs of slowing. The question before us, then, is not whether to hunt but what to hunt for. We might go looking for a deer, on advice from that cave painter; a brook trout, on advice from Robert Traver; a lion, on advice from Don Quixote; or a sale at the mall, on advice from Willard Scott. We could even sit in the woods buck-naked and pound on drums, hoping to call something in. I am not making any of this up.

With confusion so widespread in the human race, it is hard to be certain of following the right trail. Fortunately, there is a school of philosophy called cynegetics, and it never fails to distinguish between pursuits that are good, bad, or trivial. Cynegetics is Greek for hunting with a dog—most rigorous of disciplines and one of the more honest, because the dog is in charge of quality control. You cannot fool a dog, or more precisely, you can fool a dog once. After that you are fooling yourself.

If you try to stop at the mall, for example, an experienced dog will advise you to keep driving. His specialty is finding secrets in the fields and woods. He can cover ten times more miles than you or me and pick up scents a hundredfold weaker—or more likely a thousandfold. He uses these skills to detect where a grouse has walked on fallen leaves and then follow up on the clue. A few other predators are, perhaps, able to cover as much ground and smell as keenly as the dog. A very few may even have a brain that makes as much sense of the available information. But none of the others is willing to run in our pack.

A dog was, by far, the first domestic animal. She was probably a bitch pup, just a little less wild than her brothers but still a pack hunter like us humans, and therefore able to make sense of our rules. After some twenty thousand years, her relationship with us is still closer than that of any other animal. The cat sleeps by our fire too, but does not work with us; the horse works with us but does not sleep by the fire.

My dog both lives and works with me. When hunting, he finds a covey of quail and calls me to come and get what we both want. His way of calling is to stand on point, but other kinds of dogs— flushing dogs and hounds—communicate in other ways. What matters is not the breed but the fit between canine and human temperaments, because without that fit, the two cannot mesh as a team.

Personalities match best when a pup is brought up in its natural environment—a human family. Scholars have confused themselves on this point by studying dogs raised in kennels, which resemble nothing in canine evolution. To put it in Greek, pups are anthropomorphic. Translated, this means that they have human characteristics—not all of them, but enough that dog and human each understand the common ground, when understanding is given a chance. If you keep a pup in confinement, deprived of family and job, you get an impaired dog, just as you would get an impaired human. Both species hate to live on welfare payments.

If, on the other hand, you raise a dog at your hearth and give it meaningful work, it will become as close to you as any human, and in certain ways closer. Your skills and the dog's are complementary, not competitive. He becomes an extension of your personality—a piece of your consciousness that can run with the wind and stand shaking on scent. At some level the two of you merge into one hunter.

A remarkable thing happens, then. The man/dog bond is almost too close for comfort, like the link between mother and child in the night. My wife used to say that her baby's cry reached her stomach, somewhere—woke her up from deepest sleep, made her get out of bed. I snored on. Once a puppy has wriggled down into my limbic system, however, I'm with him every step. I know when he's in trouble with a fence, when he's just running around having a whee of a good time, and when he's working scent. We are chasing the same pheasant, by then, feeling the same emotions. Exactly the same. I know. We both know.

We must be hunting the right thing.

Gene Hill, an associate editor of Field & Stream, *is the author of eight books of essays on the out-of-doors. Prior to being with* Field & Stream *he was the executive editor of* Sports Afield *and a vice president, creative director of J. Walter Thompson. He has trained and field trialed better-than-decent Labrador retrievers and a couple of middling English setters. He has hunted birds and big game in a long list of places and is an eager, if not notable, clay target shooter. Fly fishing takes up what time is left, especially in tarpon and bonefish water, unless there is a chance for Atlantic salmon.*

PLAIN DOGS, SPECIAL DAYS

by Gene Hill

I've got a very soft spot in my heart for the ordinary working dog. The bird dog or retriever that doubles as house guardian, walks the kids up to the school bus and waits for them to come home, goes along on trips to the hardware store, and does what can be done about keeping the squirrels out of the attic and the rabbits out of the kitchen garden. He doesn't get much in the way of bird hunting, and the man that owns him is just about the same.

What with chores and making a living, the days in the field don't quite measure up to the hopes and dreams.

Just before the season they put in a little yard work and, with luck, an hour or so with a live pigeon or a quail or pheasant from the local game farm. Chances are that neither of them is sure they're going about this exactly the right way, but the smell of fall is in the air and there's a big red X on the calendar just a couple of weeks away.

We'll see them together on the back roads looking for just the place; the Brit or pointer or setter sitting up front making nose smears on the windshield and Himself, just as anxious, wishing he had a better gun, was a better shot, knew a perfect covert—wishing especially that he could offer old Duke all these things...all the time.

Whenever I see this pair of pilgrims I wish them their "day of days." I've been with this sort of team on a lot of occasions and much to my delight and surprise have had some honestly unforgettable days over what the usually apologetic owner calls "just your ordinary bird dog." One was in Texas and when I lavishly and honestly praised the little lemon–and–white pointer, her owner blushed and said, "I know you've seen lots and lots of better dogs and I know Dixie ain't much but she *will* find and hold birds if they're around." Well, that's all we really want 99 percent of the time anyway. Dixie had a nice gait for a walking gunner, a merry attitude, a good nose, and nice manners. She'd never make the cover of a dog book but she had more than enough style to suit me. Her owner admitted that she more or less broke herself since he didn't know much about fancy training but just needed a dog to find birds. He said that even though he had to work almost every day, he found time to put her into birds. I asked him how many birds had been shot over her and he grinned a little so I wouldn't make the mistake of thinking he was bragging, and said, "Well, maybe over a thousand." He said that this might have made up for her not having any "papers." I said I thought it might too. He asked me if I'd seen any of those big field trial dogs and I said I sure had. Then he asked, "What's wrong with my Dixie compared to them?" I told him that the only thing I could see wrong with

Dixie was that she didn't have a twin sister looking for a good home.

A lot of us, probably most of us, don't have birds in that kind of number or the time or the places. We rely on faith, good luck, and hope, and often enough they come together and we can say that wonderful phrase, "If there're birds there, she'll find them," and know it's true.

The trouble with most bird dogs are the bird hunters who own them. One dog I wanted to own belonged to a man who had absolutely no good idea of what a dog ought to be doing. He wanted to run the show, regardless of wind direction, regardless of cover, regardless of common sense. He shouted, he threatened, he waved his arms in the air and missed no chance to confuse and intimidate the dog. He'd bought the dog because he liked the way it worked for its trainer, but in two weekends he had reduced the poor thing to a neurotic mess.

Like a bird dog that "just goes out and finds birds," all an ordinary hunting retriever has to do is learn to sit, stay, and mark fairly well. If you have such a dog, you'll be surprised at what he, or she, will learn to do on its own. I believe that a lot of otherwise fine dogs are ruined, or at least curbed, by overzealous and often ill–advised training—or better—overtraining. It takes an expert to draw the line between bringing a dog along at the pace of the dog's ability rather than at a pace the owner decides is right—regardless of evidence to the contrary. Dogs are like children. They come along in fits and starts, each different, each unique. Some dogs are superb markers and can early on handle triples. Some come along slowly, and others never can do it perfectly. I don't care how good a shot you are; I can find someone better. But you're probably good enough to enjoy yourself and occasionally have a day where you're superb. And now and then have a day that you don't want to talk about. But by now you know your limitations. Why should your dog be any different? Learn the difference between what he can't do and what he won't do and direct your handling along those lines; you'll both be happier and he might just surprise you, when given a little time and understanding.

I've had a lot of retrievers and they've all been a different study. My first one was instinctively good; a far better dog than I was a trainer. She just went out and did it, often to my great astonishment. She didn't really like schooling, it seemed to bore her and when she had had enough of it she just lay down and said "enough." Another loved it and would work until everyone was exhausted. In truth she was just too much dog for me, and I never developed her potential; she belonged to a professional and I wouldn't give her up and let that happen. Another was lovable and seemingly useless until she was two years old, and then she decided that she wanted to do what the other dogs were doing and became a fine field dog.

As a now and then field trial judge I've seen too many dogs that were either not ready or not capable of repeatedly doing advanced work: long and difficult marks, intricate handling to blind retrieves, and the like. Most dogs will do something remarkable from time to time, but that doesn't mean that they are on a particular level and will stay there.

A noncompetitive dog, the one you want to take in the field and be your pal, doesn't have to be a canine Ph.D. You have to enter into the picture as a partner as much as a schoolmaster. Correct annoying faults, surely, but don't ask a dog to do things it simply can't do, whether from breeding or brains or physical ability. Most bird dogs can't run at top speed for three hours like the National champions do. You wouldn't want them to. You want a dog to work at such and such a speed and at a given range. It's possible to alter this *somewhat* but that's all. A pickup is not an Indy car.

I hate to say this but it's true: too many bird hunters don't really know what they want their dog to do. They forget that it is the dog that's doing the hunting and they are the shooter. They don't give the dog the benefit of the doubt or acknowledge that the dog might know more about cover and wind and how to work this particular area better than they do. I can say this easily because I've made all the common mistakes often and some of the rare ones more than once. One of my faults, when I was younger, was to hunt a dog too fast. I kept pushing and pushing until the dog said, literally, well if he just wants me to run through all this, that's what I'll have to do. Or I'd poke around a cover like I was looking for a lost dime until the dog, who had long ago known there wasn't anything here, got bored and went off somewhere else or came in and hung around my feet wondering what the hell I was up to.

What most of us need and get in a dog are too often different things. Obviously, if you like to potter around in the grouse and woodcock covers you don't want a rib-sprung pointer that was born and bred to quarter quail country in front a man on good horse, with an outrider along for good measure. Obvious? Sure, but it doesn't work that way as often as you'd think. One of the best bird dogs I ever hunted over was sold to me by a man who *never* hunts on foot and he couldn't stand the thought of a dog ranging out there about forty yards, no matter how letter perfect she was. A black Lab I sold as a puppy grew into one–hundred–pound rocket that was born for top-flight field-trial work. He was bred from fine trial stock and everything really came together, but he'd drive you crazy if all you wanted was a dog good with the kids or one able to bring back the odd duck from an occasional Saturday morning shoot.

If you only have time and room for one dog and you get one that isn't going to work, it's only fair that you do something about it and do it quickly. Some dogs require a firmer hand than most of us are willing or able to lay on. Others turn out so timid that only the most patient and saintlike handler can bring them around. A good breeder will work with you on this, which is another good reason to be most thorough when you go shopping and make this arrangement in advance. I know it's hard to do but I also know, firsthand, that it's harder in the long run if you don't. I once had a Brittany that was a lot more than I could handle. She was top of the line and her field work was superb, but I just wasn't tough enough to make her work for me and hunt how and where I wanted. She belonged on the south-west prairies and knew it; I wanted a choirgirl, and she longed for bright lights and the fast lane.

If at all possible, both you and your dog will benefit from its living in the house as a member of the family. You don't need forty acres to teach the basics of obedience; "sit" and "stay" work just as well in the kitchen or the den. You'll develop a closer bond, that subliminal magic that defies explanation but exists nonetheless. I suppose I flatter myself but I feel better when I have Tippy or Ben around to comfort me and want to believe that this works both ways.

Like many of you, I wouldn't hunt without a dog. The enthusiasm and joy and the feeling of partnership come, in the main, from my being there with my pal. He understands the dream and plays the leading role in the drama. He consoles me whenI'm blue and does his crazy little dance for me to show he's glad that I'm happy. I once wrote how I feel about all this and since I don't think I'll ever say it any better, I'll take the liberty of quoting myself: Nobody can fully understand the meaning of love unless he's owned a dog. He can show you more honest affection with a flick of his tail than a man can gather through a lifetime of handshakes. I can't think of anything that brings me closer to tears than when my old dog—completely ex-hausted from a full and hard day in the field—limps away from her nice spot in front of the fire and comes over to where I'm sitting and puts her head in my lap, a paw over my knee, and closes her eyes and goes back to sleep.

Jim Fergus is a freelance writer whose work has appeared in a variety of magazines and newspapers, including Newsweek, Newsday, Esquire, Outside, The Paris Review, Harrowsmith Country Life, The Denver Post, The Dallas Times-Herald, *and others. He is a field editor of* Outdoor Life *magazine, for which he writes a monthly column,* The Sporting Road. *His book,* A Hunter's Road: A Journey With Gun and Dog Across the American Uplands, *published in 1992, was a selection of the Book-of-the-Month-Club and the Outdoor Life Book Club. Currently in its third hardcover printing,* A Hunter's Road *was recently published in a paperback edition.*

When not on the road researching, writing, hunting, fishing, and living in a 1972 Airstream trailer with his yellow Lab, Sweetzer (with whom he travels upwards of 20,000 miles a year), Fergus divides his time between his home in northern Colorado, Idaho, Arizona, Florida, and points between. Whenever possible he lives with his wife, Dillon, and two other dogs, neither of them with any potential whatsoever as hunters, but good dogs nevertheless.

A DOG'S LIFE

by Jim Fergus

A Rose by Any Other Name

Let's get this one thing out of the way right off: I have the dubious distinction of owning a yellow Lab that, by general consensus among hunting friends and companions all across America, has the stupidest name ever conceived for a hunting dog. Sweetzer, she is called—named after Sweetzer Summit in southern Idaho, as I am forever explaining apologetically to those who express their thinly (if at all) disguised contempt for the name. A columnist in one of the sporting magazines even complained about my dog's name in his review of a book Sweetz and I collaborated on a few seasons ago. Indeed, one of my very best friends loathes the name so much that he refuses to use it, has actually given her another name that she must go by at his house. The affrontery! The indignity!

So let me just say this in my defense, in Sweetz's defense, in my wife's defense (not to be unchivalrous about this but actually the dog belongs to her, *she* named her Sweetzer): there are worse dog names. You don't believe me? O.K., for instance, a couple of seasons ago while bird hunting in eastern Montana, I was camped in an RV park when Sweetz and I ran into a retired gentleman from Oregon who was also out walking his dog—one of those little furry, yappy *foo-foo* dogs, which due to their compact size seem to be the dog of choice for retired couples traveling in RV's or living in condos in south Florida. (And who can blame them? Just try, as I have, to get a Lab into an RV or a condo in south Florida.) Anyway, we stopped to chat as dog people naturally will, and I quickly ascertained from our conversation and from one of many tattoos that ran up and down the man's ropy, muscular arms, that he was an ex-Marine, a drill sergeant, in fact, who from the look of him had clearly earned his living after he mustered out of the corps in some manner other than sitting behind a desk. He wore a white T-shirt and still had a Marine crewcut and though no longer young, he still possessed the strong, broad-chested physique of one who might have been lifting major appliances for the past thirty or forty years. Deciding to take the offensive and get the inevitable moment of ridicule over with, I asked the man what his dog's name was; it wasn't much of a dog, as far as I could tell, but I figured it to have a macho name—Rocky, or Buck, something along those lines. Suddenly, much to my astonishment, the ex-Marine got all bashful. "I'm almost ashamed to tell you," he mumbled.

Ashamed to tell *me*? "Hey, look," I said, "it can't be any worse than my dog's name."

"What's your dog's name?" He asked hopefully.

"My dog's name is Sweetzer," I said, steeling myself for the burst of disdainful laughter with which this information was generally greeted.

"Well, that's not such a bad name," he said, and he seemed kind of disappointed, "mine's a lot worse than that."

"Really? Well go ahead and tell me. I promise not to laugh."

And then the tattooed ex-Marine drill sergeant, a man who I'll bet in his prime could have lifted a full-sized refrigerator/ freezer all by himself, easy, actually blushed, turned downright crimson as he muttered his dog's name, barely discernible.

"I beg your pardon?" I asked, not certain I'd heard correctly.

He gathered himself up and glared at me defiantly, as I had done many times myself in defensive posture to queries about

my dog's name. "Precious," he said clearly. "My dog's name is Precious, O.K.? The wife and I named him that because when he was just a little bitty puppy, he was so damn *precious*."

"Ha!" I exclaimed triumphantly, delighted to have finally found a wimpier, more insipid dog name than Sweetzer.

"I thought you said you weren't going to laugh," the man reminded me.

"I'm not laughing," I said, quickly adding, "It's a fine name. And, in my opinion, he's still precious!"

Unfortunately, it was quite clear that Precious had never been a hunter, so, as I am repeatedly reminded by friends and acquaintances alike, I still own the stupidest named hunting dog in America.

The Things They Carry

One morning, only a few weeks after I brought the new puppy home, my wife woke up to discover that her wedding ring had disappeared off the bedside table. Being an extremely tidy and responsible person who hasn't lost or missplaced anything since maybe 1962, she immediately fingered our new family member as the likely thief. I tried to defend the defenseless little pup; she was hardly bigger at the time than, say, a plump throw-pillow with stumpy legs, and already could do no wrong in my eyes. "How could she possibly have taken your ring off the table?" I argued. "Even if she was standing on her back legs, she's hardly tall enough to reach up there. Besides," I added "we'd have heard her, and nothing else on the table is even disturbed." We searched the house all day long, from top to bottom, but the ring did not turn up.

In the wee hours of the following morning, long before dawn, I was awakened by the distinctive heaving sound that dog owners learn to dread, particularly when it occurs in the bedroom at 3:00 a.m. (Spoiled from the start, Sweetz slept in a dog bed at the foot of ours, working her way up quickly to a spot curled next to me on the human bed, until, the growth of Labs being what it is, she had eventually driven my wife to take up residency in the guest room.) I got up to see what was ailing the puppy just as the heaving reached its crescendo. There on the carpet, glittering in the moonlight, was the purloined wedding ring.

"I hope you're going to clean that mess up," my wife muttered sleepily, oblivious to the contents.

"I'll take care of it," I said, "Go back to sleep." I rinsed the ring off in the bathroom sink, dried it, and gently slid it back on the bedside table, as if the mysterious thief of the night had had an attack of conscience and returned the stolen goods. The next morning my wife slipped it on her finger without a word.

The wedding ring had to be secured now, because, although Sweetz would never again mistake it as edible, once discovered as a desirable *objet*, a collectible if you will, it would also never again be entirely safe from her burgeoning carrying fetish, its scent forever imprinted in her mind as definitively as if it had wings. And she took a similar interest in other items. Soon her bed filled with an eclectic collection of stuff: empty toilet paper rolls (which fit perfectly in her little mouth and must have seemed like small retriever dummies even before she knew about retriever dummies) would be recycled from the bathroom trash to be paraded proudly around the house for all to see. One earmark common to the canine carrier/collector is the pride they take in their hobby, the desire they seem to have for everyone to admire their stuff. Empty Dove soapboxes were another favorite to be pilfered from the trash. These she carried slipped over her lower jaw like a sheath before depositing them on the bed with her other stuff. She became particularly fond of the little fabric covered elastic bands that my wife used to pull her hair back in a ponytail. They must have felt soft and springy in the puppy's mouth and she devised a special way of pilfering them off the dressing table. She would sit casually against the table, arc her head backwards and daintily snatch the hairbands in her teeth, then stealthily make off with her booty. Soon her collection included bands in all the assorted colors, and, of course, my wife had none. "Tell that dog of yours to give me back my hairbands," my wife would demand periodically. Actually, as I mentioned, the dog was supposed to belong to her, but my secret intentions to appropriate her as a hunting dog had already been made clear. For my part, I had either read somewhere, or possibly just decided in my own mind, that retrievers are never to be punished, nor even reprimanded for carrying things in their mouths lest they begin to think that this is not a good thing for them to do. So, admittedly, I wasn't much of a disciplinarian around the house.

Soon no item even vaguely cylindrical, and in size between a chapstick tube and a small fireplace log, was safe from Sweetz's burgeoning interest in carrying and collecting. Indeed, if we happened to be looking for the former, we would be as likely to find one on her bed as in the medicine chest. And that winter when the firewood supply by the hearth became depleted and it was cold outside and we didn't feel like going out for more, we could usually count on finding among Sweetz's cache at least one log with which to stoke the dying embers.

Of course, she collected the more banal stuff as well— the obligatory shoes and socks, and the underwear pilfered from the laundry hamper. There were occassional recurrences of that awkward stage signified by the wedding ring incident—the inevitable puppy transitional period when the distinction between the activities of carrying, chewing, and swallowing are sometimes blurred. This is a stage that the bird hunter desperately hopes the dog will outgrow, and in Sweetzer's case, on one occasion it would prove nearly fatal.

We were on the road for a magazine assignment and had left the puppy in the motel room while we went out for a quick bite to eat. We returned to a grisly scene. Sweetz had gone into my wife's suitcase, removed a ziplock bag full of toiletries, opened the bag, and removed from it a full bottle of estrogen pills. Under normal circumstances this would have been nothing to worry about because pill bottles, which also have a pleasingly cylindrical shape to them, were another favorite carrying object. Unfortunately, in this case, the frustration of being left alone in a strange room had been too much for the still young dog. Somehow she managed to open the childproof bottle (putting her, I guess, on an intellectual par with a seven-year-old human), and had consumed nearly the entire bottle of pills; the remaining few were scattered on the bed, along with the bottle and the violated cap—it looked like nothing so much as the scene of a suicide attempt. We phoned the local vet and arranged to meet him at the clinic, where he gave Sweetz a shot to induce vomiting. Fortunately the pills had been ingested recently enough that only the sugar coating had dissolved from them, and no harm was done to her.

Having survived it, thankfully, the swallowing stage didn't last long and soon the carry became an end in itself. She enjoyed concealing smaller items altogether in her mouth, parading around the house with a pleased, platypus-like expression, until someone finally took notice. "You're dog has something in her mouth," my wife would remark, and I'd call Sweetz over and ask her to deposit whatever she held in my hand. Sometimes she would give up a mechanical pencil stolen from my desk and held, not crosswise, but lengthwise in her mouth, just the point peaking out from between her teeth. At other times, she might produce a single grape, taken from a bowl on the kitchen table, dropping it lightly into my palm as if offering up a precious gift. Corn-on-the-cob waiting to go on the grill was another favorite. So delicate was her grasp that she would barely dent the kernels with her teeth. Apples and oranges and even melon quarters became highly prized, and if one wasn't too squeamish about a little bit of Lab drool, they could still be rinsed off and eaten. Then one day that first spring while running with my wife on a dirt road up a canyon near our home in Idaho, Sweetz brought back a rattlesnake; fortunately it was dead, but this seemed nevertheless to augur another inauspicious, and potentially dangerous, new turn in her hobby. It also marked a whole new wildlife phase in her collecting, a phase that coincided with our retrieving work on live birds that first summer.

"Your dog has something in her mouth," my wife said one day, barely looking up from her book. Indeed, Sweetz had come in from outside and was now promenading around the room, wagging her tail, jowls compressed in their goofy platypus expression.

"Bring that here," I said. She came over to me coyly; she liked to make a bit of a game out it. "What have you got there?" Proudly, though somewhat reluctantly, she deposited a live hummingbird in my hand. I'd held them before; cupped gently in hand (and presumably in the mouth), the impossibly delicate little birds will usually remain perfectly motionless, perhaps feigning death. I didn't know how she had caught the hummingbird—who knows, maybe she snagged it right out of the air—but in any case, it seemed to me an interesting retrieve. I took the hummer outside and opened my fist. A bit damp from Sweetz' mouth, which must have seemed like Jonah's stomach to the tiny bird, it looked around as if startled, shook itself off like a wet dog, and buzzed indignantly up out of my open palm. Sweetz and I watched it away, our first, although not our last, experience with catch-and-release hunting.

"You're dog has something in her mouth," remarked my wife on yet another day.

"Bring that here," I commanded. She obeyed. "Open up and let's see what you've got there." Inside her mouth was a tiny, hairless, new-born cottontail rabbit, evidently stolen from the den; it was alive, unharmed. "I'll be damned," I said, "It's a bunny. She's got a baby bunny in her mouth!"

My wife looked at me strangely and shook her head, a look and a gesture I've grown rather accustomed to over the years. "Tell her to put the bunny back where she got it," she said.

Of course Sweetz is all grown up now, entering middle age, but she still hasn't lost her interest in collecting. For instance, I'm looking at her right now; she lies snoozing on the bed in my office, surrounded by some of her prized possessions—an eclectic collection of stuff. Her head rests on one of my shoes, which also has a sock, a tennis ball, and a chapstick secreted in it (she's learned to collect several items in one mouthful, filling a shoe for instance with smaller things.) By her chin is an empty cardboard toilet paper roll, an empty Dove soap box, and one of my wife's elastic hairbands—all perennial favorites. Against her stomach, she has deposited one of her retrieving dummies, and tucked up under her haunch is another tennis ball. Right by the tip of her nose, is my old sweat-stained orange hunting cap, sun-faded to a kind of peach color—it must certainly remind Sweetz of past days afield, and of those to come.

And now as I watch her on the bed, surrounded by her booty, her nose begins working back and forth, her eyes rolling in R.E.M., her feet and legs twitching spasmodically. Probably she's hunting in her dreams, and maybe, if I'm lucky, I'm hunting with her.

True Love

One time late in a dinner party of old bird hunting cronies who had known each other for many years, and who had seen each other through sundry personal difficulties that included marital discord, divorce, separation, illness, death, bankruptcy, and all the rest of what is frequently referred to as "real life," after everyone at the table had consumed rather too much wine, and the conversation had turned, as it naturally will to bird dogs, someone suddenly posed the, even by bird hunters' standards, incredibly immature query: "Everyone present who prefers the company of your favorite bird dog to that of your spouse, raise your hand." Snap shots all, a unanimity of hands fired up around the table—a stunningly naked group confession. Hands aloft the hunters looked at one another with growing sheepishness, as if they had all accidently fired both barrels on a covey rise of ground doves. And then, all at once, everyone roared with laughter.

Of course, it was all in fun, and it wasn't strictly true, nor was it necessarily a question that only hunters would so answer. Ask the same question of any table full of drunken dog lovers (or even sober ones) and one might expect the same response. Still, I can't help but feel that we sportsmen love our dogs *more* than does the average pet owner. And if this last statement is likely to elicit howls of protest from the toy poodle devotee, then let me qualify it, let me put it another way, and as bluntly as possible: the *quality* of the sportsman's love for his dogs is superior to that of the average dog owner. Now I can literally feel myself being pummeled about the head and shoulders by a mob of angry pooper-scooper wielding Central Park dog lovers: *We love our dogs just as much as you do!* they protest, *and what's more we love them every bit as well!*

Well, maybe so, but I still think that the quality of the sportsman's love for his dog is superior for the simple reason that the sporting dog itself is superior. (More outraged howls: *Elitist swine! Hunting dog chauvinist!*, and now the incensed mob

A DOG'S LIFE ———————————————————————————— *17*

of garden-variety house dog owners are wielding their pooper scoopers like lacrosse sticks, pelting the retreating author with their cargo of unmentionables.)

But listen, it isn't such a hard argument to make. Let me give you a real-life example: two Lab puppies from the same litter, one male, one female, go to two different owners who also happen to be old friends. The owner of the female is a nonhunter, let's say he's a poet. The owner of the male is a lifelong bird hunter, say, a novelist. Now the novelist immediately begins training his puppy as a bird dog, both for flushing and retrieving upland birds and as a retriever of waterfowl. Said novelist is a consumate hunter, and the training process, although quite specific, is at the same time rather casual and completely natural; by putting his dog in hunting situations, he is, in fact, simply reinforcing, heightening and refining centuries of genetic selection that has resulted in his dog's instinctual predisposition to find and retrieve birds. And right from the start, there is no mistaking the fact that the hunter's dog while growing daily in confidence and competence, is having a whole lot of fun in the bargain.

Now the poet, on the other hand, provides no training for his puppy, formal or otherwise, though he does take her on long daily walks through the woods and on long drives in the car. These excursions are also lots of fun for the dog, but they are without structure, specific purpose, or real challenge. Not incidentally, every day the poet also recites his morning's output of poems to his dog. This is, arguably, a somewhat less compelling activity for canines, but then who am *I* to say so? And don't get me wrong, the guy is a wonderful poet, who, I'm sure, loves his dog as much as it is possible for a nonhunter to love a dog.

Yet I still maintain that the novelist's dog is a superior creature—smarter and more imaginative, capable of more intuitive thought processes; his wits have been tested and expanded, his instincts focused and honed, his intellect heightened by use—by being required to *think*. And in the bargain he has also become a superior athlete. He has, in short, benefited from a very well-rounded education. At the same time, he and the novelist are partners in a mutual passion, not simply owner and pet, but full partners in an activity that they both love to do, were both born to do, and at which they are both quite good. This provides an incredibly strong bond between them, a bond deeper and fuller than that between the poet and his dog, who's relationship is based on...what?...a mutual love of iambic pentameter? And so it follows by this line of reasoning that the hunter loves his dog with a more informed love, a love more focused and specific and equal, in short, if one dares to qualify love—a greater, fuller, superior love. *Voila!* Now the author is finally out of range of the pooper-scooper brigade, their missiles falling hopelessly short of their intended target.

A Codicil

Here is what I mean to say, finally, about our sporting dogs: There are far more than just pets, companions and pals; they are full-time collaborators, the too-short decade or so of their lives a perfect mirror image of that same period in our own. Through the medium of our dogs we can take a surprisingly accurate measure, not only of birds killed, missed, retrieved, but also of the day-to-day events—the changes, advances and reverses of our lives, the sheer mileage—not to even mention the less tangible measure of dreams, regrets, joys, and sorrows. And each dog that passes by becomes another white cross along the side of the road, one more milestone marking our own "lonely march toward doom" as another poet once put it so well.

Paul Carson is a former newspaper reporter and columnist who is now editor of RGS, the magazine of the Ruffed Grouse Society. He learned to hunt behind hounds and still believes the baying of a pack of blueticks on hot scent should be considered classical music. But it took just one trip to a grouse covert with an old English setter to make him a bird dog convert. Ever since, flushers and pointers—some with only a vague notion of how to hunt grouse—have been part of his immediate family.

TWO TO REMEMBER

by Paul Carson

The Dog That Mourned

Hunting season is winding down for another year. To tell you the truth, I won't be sorry to see it go. Oh, I got a few birds, had some fun, communed with nature—all that stuff. But you know what was missing? Competition.

I know, I know, it's sacrilege to mention competition and hunting in the same breath. But I've got to call it what it was—the thrill and joy of being out there with the greatest competitor of them all, Ripthorn's Coverbuster.

Even now it's hard to believe that Rip was a joy. If you could dip back a dozen years to ask me what I thought of him then, I would have said, "He's a crybaby that will be the cause of me never showing my face around my former hunting buddies again."

Rip checked out just before the beginning of this past hunting season. Back in August, while the rest of us were wallowing along through a heat wave, he started ignoring the prevailing conditions. He began perking old ears and gazing expectantly at far horizons. I thought everything was going to be okay with him. He knew October was out there somewhere, and he was getting psyched for it.

His attitude was contagious, and I began to feel vibrations of excitement tickling my nerve ends. Then, on the first actually chilly morning in September, I went down to the basement, to the box of cedar chips where Rip slept, and found the black-and-white English springer curled up stiff and cold. He had died in his sleep.

The full impact of what I had lost didn't strike me all at once. It sort of crept up on me through this past hunting season as I came to realize just how much Rip's hatred of my shooting a bird contributed to the splendid times we'd shared.

There were some really glorious hunts as I would outwit Rip and get shots at ruffed grouse. Rip, of course, would become enraged each time it happened, sit down right where he was and howl for a good two minutes. But that only kindled to a deeper glow my satisfaction—it was a lot like the opposing quarterback stomping in rage if your team were to pick off a pass and run it back for a touchdown.

What I felt, however, the first time Rip went into one of his acts was far from satisfaction. I'm several light years away from being wealthy, and after manipulating the family budget to where the kids wouldn't have to go shoeless, at least in the colder months, I took the plunge and bought my first bird dog, Rip. We spent the first summer yard training. But up until pheasant season opened that year none of the gunfire he had heard was aimed at birds.

Then on opening day, Rip and I, along with a couple of my hunting buddies, were sweeping through the swampy back pasture of a friend's dairy farm. A big cackling rooster flushed skyward like a dancing flame, Rip doing his darndest to climb up after him. A crack from the nearest gun brought the bird to earth.

Rip hesitantly walked over and sniffed the pheasant while I toyed with visions of him lifting it gingerly and fetching. Instead he crouched over the bird and sent a spine-chilling howl into the autumn day. He seemed to be mourning the pheasant.

The rest of the day he sulked at my heels and whimpered. My hunting partners tried to be sympathetic, but after a while the thought of a bird dog mourning the birds got to be too much.

They started off with a few hand-muffled snickers but before long were themselves cackling, with glee.

The longest day of my life finally ended and I took Rip home and shut him in the basement. During the next few days my family avoided me as if I had hydrophobia. I will admit, I was a bit testy.

Finally, I couldn't stand sulking in the house and driving to work down back alleys to avoid people who might have heard about Rip. I had to go hunting.

I was ready to start out alone for my favorite grouse covers when the gentle-voiced mother of my children showed the considerable iron deposits in her character. She said I wasn't going hunting without Rip because the investment in him had cost her the chance for a microwave anytime in the near future. And, by golly, I was going to give him more than one chance to prove he was a hunter.

So I found myself in grouse cover with Rip. He was in his glory, quartering just ahead of me with his merry, stubby tail a wiggling blur.

We came to a ruined cabin, the walls lying about on the ground and the roof sort of rotting into a tangled mess atop the stone foundation.

Rip clambered up on the pile of timbers, stuck his head down a hole, and barked once. From beneath the pile came a scrambling rush and then a grouse burst out of a hole in the foundation's wall.

I snapped up my shotgun, but Rip was way ahead of me. He used the tumbled pile of cabin as a launching ramp and shot out into space after the climbing bird. With legs windmilling, the airborne dog rammed the laboring grouse and brought it back to the ground.

He came back with his head high and his short tail stiff out behind him to gently drop the limp form of the grouse at my feet. There was, I swear, a gloating grin spread across his face.

From then on, it was a pure and simple competition that grew fiercer and more subtle throughout the years.

He was sporting about it, I'll give him that. He hunted close, no doubt because he craved an audience for his feats. But I had to watch him like a hawk to get any indication he was making game. Usually I could tell when he'd scented a bird; he would suddenly assume an air of nonchalance as he tried to fake me out and work his way into a position where he would have the best run at his quarry.

If I could guess in which bit of cover he had pinpointed the bird, chances were pretty good I'd get there ahead of him, flushing the bird and shooting. Or I could get in position and wait until he had his try at the bird, and, if he missed, then take the shot.

But there were times I never got a chance to shoot, for Rip was out there to collect his own game, which he did often enough to make it meaningful when I got the bird instead of him. Then he would shriek and howl before going to look for another bird.

I came to learn he never held a serious grudge, at least he never bit me, and his fits of pique made my victory all the sweeter.

The Con Artist

Con artists in front of the Claysville Post Office are rare. At least I'd never encountered one there before.

But when I pulled up to mail a letter at the drive-by box one frigid February Saturday there he was limping across the sidewalk toward the car. As he hobbled along he muttered pathetically, giving me the impression someone had sent him inside to buy stamps and then as a cruel joke had driven off to let him walk 489 miles home on his three good legs. At the time, of course, I didn't know he was a con artist.

He was very well groomed, if somewhat genteelly overweight, and wore a new collar with a current tag. I wasn't quite sure what his actual predicament was because I couldn't speak Brittany, not the way he was speaking it, at any rate.

With his orange–and–white coat brushed soft and giving off the aroma of a good shampoo, I figured he hadn't roughed it enough to score very high in street smarts. And because Claysville is a little southwestern Pennsylvania town bisected by U.S. Route 40—with the post office's Stars and Stripes snapping almost directly above the eastbound lane—I decided this was no place for him to start learning about fast-moving cars.

After checking around the neighborhood to see if anyone was missing a Brittany with a bum front leg, I called the state police and got a telephone number from the dog license information they keep on file. The first hitch developed when I dialed the number and a recording informed me that particular number didn't belong to anyone.

I began to feel a tad uneasy, as if I'd surfaced in the middle of that old joke where the parents pack up and leave while the kid is away from home. In this case, substitute a Brittany named Buddy Boy for the kid. At least that's the name the police gave me from his license information.

But Buddy was no kid. As he gazed intently through the windshield from the front passenger's seat as we headed into the country, I glanced his way and saw where the gray was starting to frost his muzzle.

Everyone was a little surprised, and some more delighted than others, when we got home. Nick, our aging springer, whom I had shut in my basement office before bringing Buddy indoors, moaned in agony—which might have been because he was trying to squeeze his bulk through the crack under the office door.

Kate, the eight-month-old setter pup, almost whooped for joy. Here was another something that, figuratively speaking, wore pants.

I have a feeling, judging by the way she's been carrying on around Nick since she was a furry butterball, she would like to take up a life of wantonness. And Nick, who lost some primary parts and primal urges when the vet nipped and tucked some of his internal workings a few years ago, doesn't give her much encouragement.

For Kate, Buddy was fresh game. He hobbled into the basement, gave the pup some rigmarole about getting serious in a few months when she was older, and then homed in on Laurie with uncanny instincts. Our five-year-old will take people or leave them, but she'll take any dog, no questions asked, if it throws a sloppy kiss in her direction.

Within moments Buddy had a home for life, if he wanted it. He plopped his ample haunches in front of Laurie and lifted his gimpy leg for her inspection. He made a brave show of it, artfully interjecting a few little moans.

An afternoon of phone calls revealed the hunting fraternity of the Claysville area didn't know Buddy, and, because the license information gave only a post office box number for an address, guesses ranged from far to near as to where his owner might live. The telephone directory, furthermore, wasn't a gold mine of information on the subject. Just my luck to find a dog belonging to a recluse.

Darkness fell, and so did my spirits as I visualized myself going through the rest of my life trying to keep two old dogs

from quarreling like a couple of cranky octogenarians having at each other with shuffleboard sticks. There would also be the added challenge of trying to keep Buddy's relationship with Kate platonic.

For all my misgivings, Buddy proved a model boarder through the night, sleeping in an extra dog crate in the basement.

Sunday morning, with Nick again in my office and Kate out harassing chickadees at the bird feeder, Laurie and her mother Becky gave Buddy the run of the basement after he'd been outside to water shrubs. He launched into a long speech as he shuffled around the bottom of the stairs and then began chuffing like a little steam engine about to tackle a steep grade.

"Could be he thinks his people are up here," I called as I stepped into the shower. "Let him come up for a minute to find out they aren't, then maybe he'll settle down."

The needles of hot water on the back of my neck were just starting to work on the headache I'd acquired along with the dog when Becky squawked in outrage from the kitchen. "He's watering the kitchen table leg. Shoo! Shoo! Get out!" The last was accentuated by a slamming door. My headache rallied and clung on despite the hot water spray.

The next report was fast in coming Buddy had disappeared in the direction of the road. By the time I got dressed enough to face the frosty weather, the only thing I could see of note was Kate out under the bird feeder looking as if she couldn't decide if she would stay and repel an incoming flight of bluejays or follow her new-found love.

I gave her a third option and shoved her into the basement before making for the car. We live ten miles from town, and I could imagine Buddy trying to hobble to Claysville on three good legs, menaced all the while by highballing pickups, farm dogs with a great deal of wolf in their ancestry, and cows that were possibly littermates of the dogs.

It all flashed through my mind like the plot of a Disney movie, and I was halfway to Claysville when I realized even my grandfather's foxhound on a hot trail of his favorite quarry—deer—couldn't have covered that distance in so short a time.

When I got home Becky, muffled up in a snowmobile suit, was out in the yard waving toward the bramble field on the hillside across from our house. There was Buddy, sweeping the overgrown field at a sprightly run, snaking smoothly through the occasional clumps of hawthorn.

He disappeared into a little tuck of ground and suddenly the Oriental cussings of an outraged ringneck were leaving scorch marks across the icy morning calm. The rooster clawed for altitude then set sail for parts elsewhere with Buddy after him at a full, joyous gallop.

I caught Buddy while he was casting hopefully through a clump of brambles close to the road. He resisted all of my efforts to lead him, making out that his bum leg was now utterly wrecked.

Carrying an overweight Brittany is no picnic, but he was finally back in the basement, and for the rest of the day he went outside on a checkcord.

On Monday morning, when the world finally opened for business again, I took it as a personal challenge to find Buddy's hearth and home. A check at the county courthouse gave me the same number I'd gotten Saturday from the state police; no surprise, because the information at the police barracks is nothing more than a carbon copy of the courthouse data. But a friend at the Claysville Post Office checked the boxholder information and came up with a telephone number with a "1" where my other two sources had given me a "7." I tried the revised number and hit pay dirt. Because my handwriting is often held up to ridicule, I can sympathize with a person whose ones are mistaken for sevens. I *can* sympathize, but I don't for a while.

When we got Buddy to his home, which was about a quarter of a mile from the post office, there was an old man standing on the porch to greet us. Buddy got out of the car and limped up the walk, muttering something about being kidnaped while he was trying to get home.

"Get in the house, you old faker!" the man bellowed. Buddy scooted by him, legging along in a flawless scuttle. "Had a broken leg when he was a pup," the old man said. "But he gets on awful good when it suits him."

I sighed. Yes, I had seen Buddy getting by awful good— awful good, indeed.

Michael McIntosh is one of the world's best-known writers on shotguns and shooting. He is shotgunning columnist for Sporting Classics, Shooting Sportsman, *and* Gun Dog *and a regualr contributor to* The Double Gun Journal *and* Wildlife Art News *as well. In addition to best-selling gun books—*Best Guns, The Big-Bore Rifle, *and* A.H. Fox*—he also has written books on sporting artists Robert Abbett, David Maass, and Herb Booth.*

His love for dogs began with a pointer named Cookie, who was born just a few weeks before he was. "My mother bottle-fed us both," he says. "Probably from the same bottle, which would explain some things." For the past eleven years, his constant companion has been the sweet-faced Brittany he calls October—or Doofus, depending on what she's rolled in recently. They're growing old together in their farm in the Missouri hills, though neither one shows any real signs of growing up.

TALES FROM THE DARK SIDE

by *Michael McIntosh*

If memory serves me right, I have lived with dogs I could call my own for just about forty-three years now. With few exceptions, they have been gun dogs of one stripe or another; without exception, I have loved them all, loved them as fiercely and completely as they have loved me, shamelessly and without reserve. The roster of my dogs is fairly short—minuscule, by some standards—for I have always preferred to know them one at a time, two at the most, and nearly all have mercifully been long-lived and unprone to fatal accident.

By contrast, the list of dogs that have laid some claim on a place in my heart, however momentary the affair, is enormous and would include almost every one I ever met. I have gone out of my way to make their acquaintances all over the world, gone out of pocket to see them fed and cared for when no one else was willing, gone half out of my head with grief at each loss of a dear old friend.

Simply put, I love dogs, large or little, yeoman or sissy, working stiff or pampered pet. I have to confess, though, that I love gun dogs most of all. They like what I like, which is to poke around any shaggy piece of countryside where certain birds are likely to be found and to test our collective skills of nose and gun against their capabilities for survival and flight—exercises performed in the sheer animal exuberance of taking part, of being immersed in a world whose rhythms and mysteries are so vast that the deeper we penetrate, the more its margins fade away.

As my progress toward fifty years of being a hunter is about to come down to counting on a single hand, I can no longer tally all the dogs I've known. Some stand out sharp and clear. Others come to mind only in brief images. Many more shift and blend until I haven't a clue where one might end and another begins. I've known a few geniuses, a lot of competent craftsmen, and a handful of duds whose witlessness was mitigated only by their being lovable fools. I've known some men who deserved better dogs and some dogs who deserved better men. I've learned how easy it is to blame a dog for our own shortcomings, expecting too much and offering too little, how shamelessly we take credit that rightly belongs to them, how heart-crackingly and purely damn *good* it feels to see a piece of work pulled off with a flash of brilliance.

Fond as I am of dogs, I fancy it's not an unrealistic affection—though it certainly could be. We have a penchant for glorifying dogs beyond all the limits of reality and good sense, burdening them with fantastic presumptions of nobility and then growing disappointed and blameful when they can't possibly live up to it. We do the same to women, I'm afraid, although I'd just as soon not get into that right now. Suffice it to say, we might be better off all around if we kept our romantic notions more closely in line with the way things really are most of the time.

I can't think of a better way to illustrate just how far off the deep end we can go than simply to cite the lunkhead, whoever he was, who once observed that dog spelled backwards is god, as

if it proved something. In response, I can only point out that buzzard spelled backwards is drazzub, polecat is tacelop, and the whole thesis strikes me as being so much tihsesroh. Dogs are not gods—unless, of course, we're willing to accept gods whose shortcomings sometimes are more than a match for their virtues. Dogs are simply dogs, which is enough to ensure that their concomitant disasters are more than sufficient. If I've learned anything in all these years, it's this: no creature that breathes is capable of delivering a wider range of realities more pointedly or more inescapably than a gun dog.

Now, I don't know if I've witnessed everything a gun dog can do that's either distressing, disgusting, disgraceful, disagreeable, distasteful, or some combination of two or more. Sometimes I hope so, because I'd hate to think it could get any worse.

I'm not talking about everyday lapses like tracking up the house with muddy feet, nor even such garden-variety misbehavior as selective deafness, breaking up other dogs' points, eating birds, or barreling out of a duck blind before called upon to do so. If those were the worst things dogs were capable of, then they truly would be candidates for the pantheon. The fact is, though, they are capable of much worse—acts of a magnitude to make saints fall a-cursing, behavior so vile and proclivities so foul as to gag a vulture at the very thought. Like the thorn beneath the rose, the dark side of the dog looms ever near the surface and manifests itself not so much when you least expect it but rather when it's least convenient, most embarrassing, or in some way certain to have maximum effect.

The fundamental themes that govern this shady realm are remarkably few. Perhaps this is because dogs are essentially simple creatures—and possibly because those who insist upon living with them are too. At any rate, these themes offer means as good as any for organizing a survey. In the interest of keeping this both accurate and in manageable proportion, the incidents I shall use by way of illustrating the points are strictly from my own experience or from reports by people I know to be reliable. Hard as it may be to believe, some men have been known to take liberties with the facts when relating dog stories, whether about their own dogs or others'. What you're about to read, though, is absolutely true, much as I wish most of it wasn't.

Gastrointestinals, Upper

Strictly speaking, dogs are carnivores, just like their original ancestor, the wolf. Somewhere in the long evolutionary descent from *Canis lupus*, however, *Canis domesticus* acquired a gene, possibly several, that expanded its gustatory horizon considerably. The present-day dog is omnivorous in the broadest sense of the word, which is made up of two Latin words—*omnis* or "all" and *vorare* or "devouring." Together, they denote an organism willing to consume anything, and if you looked it up in an illustrated dictionary, you'd find a picture of a sporting dog.

Exactly which breed wouldn't really matter, although among the ones I've known, the most truly catholic tastes have belonged to setters, Brittanies, and Labrador retrievers. Sorting the big-leaguers from the amateurs isn't easy, but I'd have to give Burly a slight edge on all the rest. Burly was a big black Lab who belonged to an old friend of mine. He was a grand hunter and fearless retriever. He also was a first-rate companion—usually.

The thing about burly was his appetite, both in quantity and variety. He was the only dog I ever knew who truly would eat *anything.* Which was fine so far as dog food and table scraps were concerned; we never had to go out of our way to keep him happy with what he was fed. The problem was all the stuff he'd find for himself, and even that would have been okay if his digestive system had been a match for his taste, or lack of same.

If I really put my mind to it, I probably could remember one or two trips that ended without Burly throwing up in the back of Jim's station wagon, but none occur to me right off the top of my head. And it never was just some little wad of green grass, like every other dog hurls up now and then. No, when Burly unloaded, you just had to marvel that a mere eighty-five-pound dog could hold sixty pounds of dead fish, road-kill possum, deer guts, or whatever else he'd polished off while nobody was looking.

You could tell it wasn't going to be any dainty little burp just by listening. He'd suddenly stand up, pace back and forth a couple of times to find the exact geographical center of the cargo compartment, and then give forth a chorus of rumbling and churning that sounded like a volcano giving birth to New Zealand. This would culminate in the delivery of some wet, steaming, stinking mess that invariably arrived before Jim could get the car stopped alongside the road. Pulling over always gave old Burl the idea that we weren't through hunting yet, so he'd charge up to the front seat and give me one or two good slurps up the side of my face before I could fend him off. Nobody who ever went hunting with Burly had to ask twice why Jim carried an old shovel in the car.

On one occasion I wish I could forget, he even managed a double-header. Jim had moved to western Iowa by then, and I was up for a long weekend with pheasants. We let Burly out of his kennel the first morning, and he dashed around the house to air out. While Jim got the last of his gear loaded, I walked around to see if Burly was ready and met him coming the other way, just finishing breakfast, which in this case was a full-grown squirrel that he'd either caught fresh or found in the street out front.

Either way, it was impressive. I guess he didn't want to waste any hunting time, because he was in the process of swallowing the damn thing whole, and when I came along it was all down except one hind leg and the tail. Burl sort of humped up, took a couple of mighty heaves, and even those disappeared, tail and all. Not for long, though. It all came back about twenty minutes later.

I don't know what it was he got hold of that afternoon; I'm not even sure a histologist could have made any sense of it, although he certainly would've had plenty to work with.

The last time I hunted with the old boy before he died, we parked the car next to a creek, which Burly naturally had to investigate while we uncased our guns. We could hear him still splashing around as we started off, so Jim whistled to get him moving. And he came lumbering up the bank happily chewing on what I took to be a muskrat, judging from the tail.

"Burl's eating a muskrat," I called over to Jim.

Jim kept on walking. "That son of a bitch. There's probably a Number Four Victor trap on the other end of it." He sighed. "We'll find out on the way home."

I never thought I'd meet Burly's equal—and I still haven't, really—but my Brittany October is no slouch when it comes to omnivorousness. Living on a farm as we do, she's developed a fine taste for cowflop, relishes the odd placental repast at calving time, and come fall, has an infallible knack for finding the gut pile where my neighbor field-dressed his deer.

This wouldn't be so bad if she could just keep it down, but as with Burly, her stomach has better sense than her head. Except for once when she was a pup, she's never tossed her cookies in the car, but I haven't found that to be any particular comfort when I wake up in the middle of the night to the sounds of imminent eruption—or step barefoot into the results next morning on the rare occasions when she's quiet about it.

Whenever she barfs up some godawful mess, I send her straightaway outdoors. I realize it's too late by then, but it makes me feel better to do something just in case there's more. I did that one night, and in the few minutes it took me to clean things up, she wandered out by the barn and got crossways with a skunk. At least she didn't eat it.

Possibly the most unusual thing I've ever seen a dog eat was a little package consumed and subsequently returned by a setter who belonged to my old pal Spence. We were hunting grouse in Minnesota one fall, sharing a motel room. Spence got up in the middle of the night, stepped in something, and awakened most of the local population in the process of explaining acceptable behavior to his dog. Sam the setter was not known for this sort of thing—and I didn't have anything else to do at the moment, anyway—so I asked what she'd eaten. Spence took a look and said he wasn't sure, so I had a look, too.

Nearly as we could tell, it was his underwear.

Intraspecific Infelicity

One of the things in this life that I never asked for but got anyway is a strange knack for being nearby when two dogs decide to try tearing one another limb from limb. Rarely is one of the combatants mine, since I haven't had a male gun dog in more than twenty years, so I really don't understand why I'm always the one closest to the action. Just lucky, I guess.

I do know that I have little patience with dog fights and even less with the hammerheaded types that seem to make careers out of starting them. I am therefore apt to take draconian measures.

Water, I find, is a splendid tool for sorting out a donnybrook. I discovered this one day when two Labradors began disputing ownership of a dead duck in the bottom of a boat. (These fools had just spent four hours together in the same blind without raising an eyebrow or a hackle. Besides, the damn duck was *mine*, but try to tell that to a dog.) They were in opposite ends of the boat, and I had one foot in and one in the water when they met more or less between my legs and started snarling at one another. I grabbed the nearest collar, lost my balance, dragged the dog over the gunwale, and somehow managed to get him underneath me before I hit the water. I know it sounds amazing, but holding a Labrador's head underwater for about five minutes makes him lose all interest in fighting.

I witnessed a really clever variation on this once in South Dakota, when somebody else happened to be closest to the fray for a change.

There were three of us, hunting sharptails, and two dogs — a handsome setter and an equally handsome Brittany who also happened to be one of the dumbest dogs I ever met. This specimen was competent enough, but he could make the proverbial bucket of rocks look like a Rhodes scholar. The two dogs hadn't met one another before, and by the end of the second day, it was obvious that the setter, also not overly burdened with brains, was just biding his time before starting a fight.

The sun was about half a gun-barrel's length above the western horizon. We had our birds dressed and packed away and were toasting sundown from the tailgate of the Suburban, parked atop a rise in that great, gorgeous sweep of sky and grass. Both dogs had been repeatedly admonished for their interest in the gut pile and, being dogs, were doing everything they could to circumvent their orders. They weren't even paying much attention to each other, until they met nose to nose with fresh grouse guts between them.

It was just the straw the setter was waiting for, and in about two seconds he had hold of the Brittany's ear and was settling in to punch some tickets. Without a moment's hesitation, the Brit's owner leaned over, tilted the setter's head up as delicately as a midwife handling a newborn, and poured half a can of beer right down his nose. End of fight. The setter was still snorting up the odd gobbet of foam next morning and couldn't smell birds worth a damn, but it turned out to be the pleasantest day of the trip.

On the whole, there's nothing funny about a dog fight until it's over, but I did see one that almost put me on my knees. It happened at a duck club in the Missouri River bottoms and involved two splendid young Labs and a newspaper sportswriter I used to hang out with in my teaching days.

Bill Bennett, whose name will come up again before we're through with this, is a man who should never even have owned a picture of a dog. He loved them, but they were his Nemesis. He was, for instance, the only man I've ever seen knocked flat on his face in a puddle of his own urine by a dog—but that's another story for another time. The fight I'm thinking of came after he bought the Labrador he named Ebony of Nghaerfyrddin, or some equally inscrutable Welsh word that translated as "black dog with tail." Don't ask me why.

Even as a yearling pup, Ebby, as we called him, was magnificent, big and sleek and strong, and he showed all the promise of becoming a first-rate hunter. The day we shot at Greenhead Farm, we showed up about ten minutes late and found a local physician in our blind. While he very graciously apologized for having misread the blind assignments on the clubhouse wall, his dog, who was somewhat older than Ebby and grouchy as a Cape buffalo with a case of jock itch, growled and snarled. I was not unhappy to see him led away across a field of cut corn.

We gave neither of them a thought until the end of the day, when the good doctor winged a mallard that sailed way out into the corn before going down. Since we had a better view of where it fell than he did, I suggested we go help him retrieve it. Bill put Ebby on a leash, and we waded across our pool and into corn stubble almost knee-deep with the slick, gluey northwest-Missouri mud that is a major factor in what holds the world together. Miserable stuff to walk in.

Doc and his dog were out of their blind, too, headed down the field, and when the Lab saw us coming, he wheeled around and charged straight for us. He wasn't making very speedy headway, but we couldn't, either, so I told Bill to get a good grip on the leash and I'd try to stop this maniac before he reached Ebby.

It almost worked. I got my fingertips on his collar but he ducked his head and I lost him. In the next instant, he bowled into Bill and Ebby, and all three went down in one massive tangle of arms, legs, dogs, flying mud, snarling, snapping, and half-coherent shouting.

Even if he hadn't had the leash wrapped around his wrist, Bill was as helpless against the mud as a turtle on its back. The whole pile kept rolling over and over, although somehow Bill managed to stay mostly on the bottom. For all the uproar, the dogs were scarcely touching one another, but between them they were literally stomping poor Bill into the mud. Everything he tried to say ended up choked off in midphrase—which was just as well, because none of it was fit for tender ears anyway.

It was a great show, and I enjoyed as much as I dared, but finally it was clear that I either had to do something right then or drag Bennett's carcass out of the field later. Big as the dogs were, they were flyweights compared with him, so I waded over and grabbed the first collar that came to the top of the heap. Mercifully, the other dog was wearing it. By the time I got the collar twisted into a passable form of tourniquet and managed to turn Old Crusher's attention from trying to fight to trying to breathe, Doc came slogging up, red-faced with exertion, eyes the size of teacups. I handed over his dog, and the last we saw of them, they were headed back for the clubhouse, Doc delivering a very loud lecture on aspects of Labrador parentage that I'm sure aren't listed anywhere in the Field Dog Stud Book.

On the way home, Bill rehearsed a similar dissertation that may have included some observations on my own ancestry, but I'm really not sure. It's hard to understand a man who's trying to talk and spit at the same time. Besides, all I did was suggest that if he ever got tired of journalism, he could have a great career in mud wrestling.

Commedia Sexualis

I'm sure everybody's heard the old story about the young man, invited for the first time to Sunday dinner with his girlfriend's parents, who drops a piece of food in his lap and to divert attention while he retrieves it, looks out the window and says, "Well, my heavens, look at that," pops the morsel back onto his plate, realizes that everyone is glaring at him, and looks for himself—to see two dogs mating on the lawn.

This is not a true tale, but rather a piece of modern myth, like the Cadillac convertible filled with fresh concrete or the lady who attempts to dry her French poodle in a microwave. But like all myth, it bespeaks a fundamental truth, because whatever else dogs may be guilty of, sexual inhibition is not among them. For the most part, this is an admirable, if somewhat clownish trait. Where it tends to go wrong is when some backyard breeder gets involved because he wants a pup out of Old Bolter. (In ninety-nine cases out of ten, the bird-hunting world would be vastly better off if Old Bolter's gene pool were drained, paved over, and used as a toxic-waste site, but that's another matter.)

Generally speaking, these liaisons quickly turn to comedies of error. Sometimes the dogs are the principal players, and sometimes it's the people. I knew one chap who made his garage into a love nest for a male Brittany (his) that hadn't the foggiest idea what he was supposed to be doing. When Charlie looked in a while later, he found the female sound asleep and the male busily servicing his water bucket.

Another guy I know, fearing that the female in question was going to pass out of estrus before his male could get the job done, turned the matter over to his vet and then promptly departed on a hunting trip, leaving his wife to see that things went as planned. What he didn't know was that in vitro fertilization is not widely practiced on dogs. The vet later described to me a scene you might find in some Mexican porno movie—the wife holding the female, some teenage girl who was the veterinary equivalent of a candystriper holding the male, while the vet took matters literally in hand. And none of it worked because the two women were so busy trying to look everywhere but in front of them. I've always figured the happy ending, such as it was, came about solely because the wife didn't know any divorce lawyers.

Another gentleman of my acquaintance had a male pointer he wanted to breed and arranged the services of a well-pedigreed female from a friend. When the friend called one Saturday morning in late September to announce that the female was ready, he drove across town to pick her up, taking the male along. As it turned out, she was a bit more ready than anyone realized, and by the time Tom got stuck in the traffic surrounding the local high-school homecoming parade, the dogs were well engaged in the back of his pickup. Some of his friends later presented him with a special award for having the most unusual float.

Finally, there was the time I went grouse hunting in northeastern Iowa with a couple of guys, one of whom had a male Brittany and the other a female setter that had just gone out of heat. We drove up in one chap's old Mercedes, which naturally had no place for crates, so the dogs rode in the back seat. All during the drive and the first afternoon's hunting, they paid little attention to one another.

We got showered that evening, asked about a good local restaurant, and were directed to a dinner-theatre supper club on the edge of town. The parking lot was empty when we got there, so we parked right in front. Our table was butted up against a front window, and when the waitress came back to serve our drinks, she looked out, did a double-take, and said, "Are those dogs?"

We looked and, sure enough, they were—ours, going at it in the back seat like two kids at a drive-in movie. Not knowing quite what else to do, we ordered another round of drinks.

By this time, the dinner-theatre crowd began to arrive. I don't know what the production was to be, but it definitely was something of interest to the geriatric set, because about twenty carloads of blue-haired ladies showed up and every last one had to totter over to our car to see the nice doggies. And every last one got a good look, spun around on her heels, and marched away stiff-backed as a colonel on parade. Once inside, I'm sure they thought they'd been invaded by perverts in the form of three men sitting by the window and choking to death laughing. We didn't stay to see the play.

Interspecific Infelicity

Dogs that fight with one another are annoying enough; those that tangle with other animals are usually disasters. I'm not thinking here of such mundane irritations as porcupines or housecats nor even skunks (although one skunk episode from my experience certainly qualifies; more about that in another section); what I have in mind is the kind of completely gratuitous nonsense that makes you want to grasp your gun like a baseball bat and line-drive some blockheaded mutt right over the left-field fence.

Actually, I know a man who tried just that one time. He and his big male pointer were hunting pheasants on a farm in western Iowa. He'd worked his way around a field and was nearing the farm buildings when pandemonium broke loose somewhere up ahead. Hurrying to the scene, he found his dog attacking a goat that was tethered to a tree outside a little shed. Having gone to some effort to find good hunting grounds and seeing his welcome wearing thinner by the second, he took his Winchester 21 by the barrels, charged up, and aimed a mighty swing. Unhappily, he missed the dog—also, fortunately, the goat—and smashed his gunstock to matchwood against the tree.

In the days before he bought Ebby, Bill Bennett had a nice young female Brittany who was a dandy quail dog. Prospecting one Saturday morning, he knocked on the back door of a farmhouse and was making good headway toward getting permission to hunt when his dog trotted up bearing a surprised-looking Leghorn hen. She had a wonderfully soft mouth, so the bird wasn't harmed in the least. Bill turned an intense shade of scarlet, grabbed the bird, and whacked his dog over the head with it.

Which killed the chicken dead as a hammer.

He looked at it and then at the farmer, who hadn't said a word since the whole scene began, and handed it over.

"I expect you'll want to dress this for dinner," he said. "And would you mind if maybe I came hunting some other day?"

Few breeds of men are as taciturn as north-Missouri farmers. "Son," he said, holding the now-limp fowl by the legs, "why don't you come back Friday. I was *plannin'* to kill chickens then."

Aromatica

Sometimes I look at my dog, a stunningly beautiful creature who is the product of bloodlines as classic as Brittany blood can be, and wonder what exactly we think we've accomplished: umpteen generations of careful breeding to arrive at an animal whose greatest joy is break dancing in cow manure?

I know all the genetic blueprints that prompt dogs to roll in foul-smelling matter. What I don't know is why, or more to the point, why still. It isn't as if Tober has to cover her own scent in order to go off in the woods and successfully scrag a deer to get something to eat. She couldn't catch one if her life depended on it, or kill one even if she could catch it, and she's never gone a day in her life without a healthy ration of good, nutritionally balanced food served up right on time—so why the hell does she insist on smelling like a buzzard's crotch?

To me this is one of the world's greatest mysteries and it probably is so because my aging puppy is one of the world's great practitioners of draping herself in an aura of stench. I've seen her turn from orange and white to a uniform brown in just one trip through a pasture. Just the other day, she went on a binge of such enthusiasm that one ear was packed completely full of cowflop. It has occurred to me more than once that I should have named her Meadow Muffin instead of October First.

At other times she has come to the door wearing essences of everything from rotting flesh to coyote urine to skunk musk to stuff I couldn't possibly identify except that it just smells awful. Perhaps what bothers me most is her utter lack of contrition; she loves it and clearly expects me to love it, too.

I suppose any dog is apt to roll in something vile once in a while, although I've known a few that seemed to have no interest in such activity. On the other hand, some, like mine, can't seem to live without it. Maybe it has something to do with the keen desire for hunting that we have taken such pains to preserve and enhance in the gunning breeds, or maybe it's just downright perverseness.

In any event, gun dogs probably have more opportunities for this sort of thing than most others do, and while some level of stink is pretty much routine, it sometimes gets entirely out of hand.

Wendy, for instance, once got involved in the second-worst case of rolling I ever knew. Wendy was a young, exuberant black Lab who, on a grouse hunting trip in northern Minnesota, rolled on a dead skunk.

I don't know if you've ever smelled a dead skunk, but if you haven't, you don't want to. The difference between a dead skunk and a live one is roughly the same as the difference between a live skunk and Chanel No. 5. It's enough to make a maggot retch.

Anyway, Wendy found *Mephitis mephitis* remains somewhere in the woods and coated herself with it from chin to rump. There was no place to clean her up except the bathtub in our motel room, so we were faced with the additional challenge of getting the job done in a way that left the place livable. We opted for tomato juice as the first mode of attack and literally cleared the shelves at the local Red Owl. I've since learned a much better approach, which is to mix tomato juice with liberal doses of vodka and use it for moral support while treating skunk stink with white vinegar, but I didn't know this at the time—or at least not the vinegar part.

Anyway, with the tub about half full, the bathroom looked like the set of a third-rate chainsaw movie, and we took turns laving Wendy, working in shifts just slightly shorter than the maximum span in which each of us could hold our breath. Finishing off with two big bottles of shampoo ameliorated the situation to the point where Wendy was tolerable company so long as she stayed in the back of the truck while we stayed in our room and didn't breathe too deeply.

The worst case of rolling I know occurred on a quail hunting expedition in north Missouri. Mercifully, I was not present, but

I got the story from an eyewitness. It seems that two members of the party overindulged in the consumption of beer one night and upon arriving at the hunting ground next morning were both taken with a sudden, urgent need to find a men's room with minimum delay. Being where they were, the grader-ditch offered the only option, using their car—a nearly new Suburban—as a screen against the chance of any passers-by. Thus presently relieved, they all went off a-hunting.

Back at the car in late afternoon, they set about field-dressing their birds. Left for a while to their own devices, the dogs, two Brits and a setter, found the morning's latrine, practiced some zealous gymnastics on the site and then hopped into the back of the 'Burban. By the time anyone realized what was happening, they'd done what every dog does when loose inside a vehicle— which is to say, explored every inch and tested the comfort level of every seat. It was not, I'm told, a scene fit for small children or the faint of heart.

The same day I heard this story, October came in from some cow-diving and was thoroughly taken aback when I gave her a biscuit for being a good girl. I never did tell her why, and I'd appreciate it if you wouldn't, either.

Gastrointestinals, Lower

Regardless of what a dog eats, anything that makes its way past the stomach is going to reappear sooner or later. This simply is a fact of life and isn't any particular problem unless you keep a large number of dogs or restrict one to a small space. Even at that, the worst thing likely to happen is for a dog to step in its own waste and then jump up on you, but teaching a dog not to jump on people is so easy and so fundamental to good manners that anyone who gets foot-wiped by his own dog deserves it.

Coprophagia can be a problem, mainly because it promotes horrible breath, but I believe it is most often a sign of some dietary deficiency, which isn't the dog's fault.

To my thinking, the most disagreeable product of lower gastrointestinal activity is gaseous rather than solid.

Down here in the Ozarks, asking whether a fat dog farts is the equivalent of enquiring if the Pope is Catholic or if a pig's butt is made of pork. The answer, of course, is yes; fat dogs fart. So do skinny dogs, old dogs, young dogs, and especially, gun dogs. This often is directly related to an appetite for carrion and cow pies, but I've known some dogs who could manufacture an endless supply of noxious gas on a diet of cornflakes. My father had one of those once, a big pointer who always got to ride home on the front-seat floorboard. This was in the days when automobile heaters were boxlike units installed under the dash on the passenger side, and when old Boy cut loose a measure of toxic emission, the heat and fan combined to create an atmosphere that could make your eyes water.

As with other things dogs do that result in noisome odors, the culprits themselves don't even seem to notice, which I find perennially amazing for animals whose stock in trade is their sense of smell. But I don't think obliviousness is truly the case. Waldo, my old farm dog, was a great farter in his later years, and when he'd cut one, I had only to look at him. His face would take on a sheepish expression and he'd wag his tail in an apologetic way. It isn't that dogs don't notice; they just don't care.

Moreover, I can scarcely remember ever smelling a dog-fart outdoors, which suggests some element of free will at work. October, now entering her own later years, is becoming a world-class gas-passer herself, and she clearly has some favorite times to practice. She likes evenings, when she can catch Susan and me sitting together somewhere, and late nights, especially nights when she's sleeping in her own bed, which is on the floor next to my side of ours.

Intensities naturally vary according to what miserable thing she might have eaten earlier, but in top form she can lay down a barrage that brings even me, who could snooze peacefully through the apocalypse, wide awake and gasping for fresh air.

At first, I thought she was doing this in her sleep, but after a few episodes that took place while I was still awake, I noticed that every attack is invariably followed by the sound of my dear old girl heaving a deep, heartfelt sigh of utter bliss and contentment.

I'm not entirely sure, but I think I've even heard her snicker once or twice.

As I said at the outset, I truly do love dogs, although it hasn't always been an easy affection to maintain. If, like mine, your canine mileage amounts to something over half our allotted threescore and ten, then all this probably has rung some familiar bells—as it would for any hunter of any time since man and dog first set out together in search of game. In his diaries covering the first fifty years of the nineteenth century, the great English sportsman Peter Hawker includes this note, cryptic and yet perfectly clear: "Finished my day with shooting the dog, at the express desire of Mrs. Hawker, and to the great satisfaction of all who were with us."

If by chance you're a more recent convert, perhaps working with or even anticipating your first gun dog, then you probably still harbor some romantic notions tinged with firelight and pipesmoke, the amber glow of good malt whisky and a pair of loving eyes gazing up by your side. Cling to these, and cherish them, because you're going to need them, sooner or later.

John Barsness was born and raised in Montana, where his grandparents homesteaded, and he shot his first game bird as soon as legally possible. With his wife, the writer Eileen Clarke, he lives on a trout stream in an obscure part of the southwestern quarter of the state. He's never held a real job for a whole year, instead devoting his life to hunting, fishing, and gazing at long vistas. In addition to writing for a number of national magazines, *including* Gray's Sporting Journal, Outdoor Life, Sports Illustrated, *and* Sports Afield, *he's presently a contributing editor of* Field & Stream *and* Petersen's Hunting. *His books include* Hunting the Great Plains, Montana Time: The Seasons of Trout Fisherman, *and* Western Skies: Bird Hunting on the High Plains and in the Rockies. *Though he has shot wild birds over a dozen breeds of pedigreed hunting dogs, a half-dozen accomplished mongrels, and dropped a francolin flushed by a baboon in Africa, his own dogs have been Labrador retrievers. He sees no reason to change and is working heartily toward an opinionated old age.*

A ROUGH SHOOTING DOG

by John Barsness

The British have a term for what Americans do when we bird hunt. They call it "rough-shooting," meaning we stomp around in the woods and fields—as opposed to standing in a blind or butt with a gun handler reloading our matched Woodwards as red-legged partridge fly by like skittish kamikaze. I gather this term is not exactly an honorific, and is often used to describe the sporting habits of not only Americans (who on frequent occasions use, gasp, repeating shotguns) but the Irish. What the Irish have to say about the sporting habits of the Brits is not appropriate for this treatise.

Over here the dichotomy between classes of bird hunting is not so vast, though as land disappears into the maw of the mall, some of our rough-shooting seems to have become more stylized. I was born, raised, and still live in Montana and have watched the process occur even here. Why, just down the road in the Gallatin Valley there are several shooting preserves, offering stocked pheasants and chukar, and dog clubs where the members stand around on Saturday injecting the little thrill of electricity into their pointing dogs' necks. All of these gentlemen use double guns, and while none as yet wear ties while chasing Hungarian partridge, at least one adds the subtitle "Esq." to his name.

Luckily, when I was growing up out here three decades ago, there were no such role models around. The primary method of bird hunting was to drive around on logging roads and shoot ruffed grouse with a .22 rifle, or take their heads off with a .30-06 while out after elk. My father was antibird hunting, not because he didn't like to kill or eat them, but because unlike shooting mule deer, it wasn't cost efficient. He was an English professor but had grown up during the Depression on a Montana homestead and still saw any sort of game in utilitarian terms. If pheasants had come wrapped frozen in threes down at Heeb's Grocery then he might have been interested, particularly during weekend sales.

My first real live sporting idol was a friend of my father's, one of his fellow professors who lived in the house across the alley from us. He killed his deer every year, had a genuine six-point elk head sitting out in his garage, and caught trout on flies he tied himself. When pheasants first grew numerous enough to hunt in the valley, around 1960, he bought a bolt-action 20-gauge, then walked through a local cattail slough until a bunch of roosters flew. He was as good with the 20-gauge as his "sporterized" Springfield, and as the birds got up he killed a limit of three with three shots, afterwards declaring "there wasn't much to pheasant hunting." My father used this as further evidence in his antibird campaign.

So my main education came from outdoor magazines, books like *The Old Man And The Boy,* and even worse. I was under the impression that there were two kinds of bird dogs in the world. The first were not only able to do mathematics with day-old scent (E+nose=quail/12 ga.) but could run all day, hold a point as long as the Statue of Liberty, and save drowning babies. The second type ate chickens and pecan pies, busted coveys, and belonged to young boys who didn't wear ties and probably never would.

So it was something of a surprise to meet my first real live bird dog. This was a Brittany spaniel that belonged to a student of my father's, who lived in a tiny cabin in one of the local canyons so he could hunt deer and grouse and catch trout. (Somewhat typically, he was from New York City. Montana kids usually wanted to move to the city, meaning Spokane.) I really didn't have much interest in bird hunting, but the student invited me out one day during my first legal hunting season, at age twelve. We each carried a double gun, quite by accident, and followed Duchess the Brittany up a side draw in the canyon. This was before Brittanies had been bred into schizophrenic imitations of Southern pointers and learned to run like hell; Duchess meandered quite placidly from side to side across the bottom of the draw, almost always in sight, once in a while flash-pointing at the bottom of an aspen.

Twenty minutes up the draw she pointed hard, nose uphill. The student pointed too, at the dog, and pantomimed for me to move up behind her. While I did, brain full of adrenalin and sixty-three *Old Man And The Boy*s, Duchess held as steady as the mounted black bear in the window of the Stockman's Bar. Then I was right behind her, and nothing happened. No thunder-flush, no gray ghost ripping through the trees, none of the stuff I'd read about. Then Duchess tilted her head up a little, looking at an aspen a few feet away, and barked.

I had never read of this. It was as if my phys ed teacher had lined us up for calisthenics and then recited Robert Frost. The student walked up beside me, shotgun ready, looking up in the tree. "Get 'em, Dutch," he said, and Duchess leaped up and bounced her front paws against the aspen. A ruffed grouse fell out of the top, gliding almost silently across the coulee, until the student's shotgun went boom and the grouse fell in the leaves.

Almost thirty years later, Duchess is still the most useful single hunting dog I've ever known. In today's terms, when Hungarian-loony Western hunters like their Brits to cover counties as large as Delaware in a morning, she would be considered almost as slow as Dan Quayle. When she decided the wisest move was to break point and bark, she did so, though never without a gunner in range. She also was quite passable in a duck blind, though Canada geese were a little large for a forty-pound dog. She hunted every legal bird out here, which includes five different grouse, Huns, pheasants, snipe, and ducks, and always seemed a little smarter in that capacity than any human she ever accompanied. If doves had been legal then I suspect she'd have figured a way to toll them.

The next rough-shooting dog I met belonged to my grandfather-in-law, an old Sioux Indian from the Fort Peck Reservation in northeastern Montana. Ben was not only a hunter and angler of nearly seventy years experience, but a highly practical scavenger as well. When he visited the local landfill, odds ran about fifty-fifty that he'd come back with more than he took. One day he returned with a black puppy that someone had abandoned. He claimed it was a Labrador retriever, and indeed there may have been some in there because Suzy Dump (as he named her) retrieved anything that fell down, including the walleye and channel cats Ben pulled out of the Missouri River.

But she specialized in putting sharptailed grouse and pheasants out of the thick buffalo berry and wild rose thickets of the reservation. From the first of September on through December, these are the favorite houses of those birds. Ben showed me how to tell when they'd set up shopkeeping in a particular thicket, pointing out the "chicken trails" the birds pushed underneath the branches and grass, creating archways not unlike those found in old Mexican cathedrals. By then Ben was too old to walk the longer coulees, so he'd drop me and Suzy Dump off at one end, then drive his pickup to the other, anywhere from a half-mile to two miles away, and wait for us to drive birds toward him, picking off what we could along the way.

Suzy's technique was to push her way along a chicken track until she'd chased all the birds into the thickest part of the brush. Early in the season many of the birds would flush quite readily, and I'd often have a full game bag by the time I met Ben, but later—particularly during pheasant season—they grew more wary and adept at worming their way like feathered ferrets under the matted grass and wild roses. Then Suzy used her patented Heinz 57 technique, named not only for her heritage but her motion: she jumped up and down on top of the matted roses like a newly opened bottle of steak sauce some giant was trying to unplug. Often this was in brush shoulder high to me, and all I could see were her pointy ears at the apex of each jump, flipping skyward like two lapping black tongues before she disappeared again. The cover was so thick that sometimes I could hear a bird starting to claw its way out for what seemed like a full minute (and may have been six or seven seconds) before it appeared, looking as nonplussed and disheveled as a banker suddenly thrust into a mud wrestling contest.

But unlike Duchess, Suzy Dump was a specialist, not much use at anything else. As a waterfowl dog she lacked attention, quite often abandoning the bird in the last thirty feet of the retrieve, which in the Missouri River rendered her quite useless. She was very attentive to whomever she hunted with, so much so that on one cold November day, when Ben and I were jump-shooting a series of stock ponds for mallards and whatever else we might find, she almost drowned me. We sneaked to the edge of one cattail-rimmed pond and when six mallards jumped, killed one in the pond and one on the land.

The one on the land was no problem, but the cattail margin was frozen, the ice just thick enough that Suzy couldn't break it. I wore hip boots and decided to break trail to the edge of cattails and open water, so she could swim out, get the duck, and, I hoped, bring it all the way back. (By that point in our career, I always carried a stout spinning rod and several huge treble hooks to snag any ducks Suzy abandoned in midretrieve, so field-trial behavior wasn't necessary.) When I entered the water Suzy came with me. The bottom was typical black muck, and by the edge of the cattails I was up to my ankles in ooze and almost to the top of my hip boots in icewater. I tried to step aside to get out of Suzy's way but was stuck. She was swimming in a narrow track through the ice and couldn't back up, so she swam right up my jeans pockets. We both went down and experienced a new low in physical sensation. On my life list I'd put falling into thirty-two-degree mudwater somewhere be-tween being kicked in the crotch and a Scotch hangover. The recovery period was somewhere between, too; when we slogged back to the truck Ben just said, "The next pond's a couple miles. You'll have time to dry out." Oddly enough, both Suzy and I did, partly because we had to wait a half-hour for the mallard to drift to the dam end of the pond where she did retrieve it. That is rough-shooting at its finest.

There have been other rough-shooting dogs over the years, ranging in skills and heritage between Duchess and Suzy Dump. One was Norm Strung's Boykin spaniel, Pistol, who went along on beach expeditions and learned to dig clams. Another was a German shepherd who not only flushed and retrieved pheasants but on one occasion ran down a wounded deer, throttled it, and came back to lead his master to the deer. ("Search, Lassie, and destroy!") Bill DeShaw has a Brittany that is the closest genetic throwback to Duchess I've seen in this age of jet-powered pointing spaniels. She's come up with yet another approach to rose-and-grass thickets; she gets down on her belly at pheasant height and points under the brush. Bill waits until the brush quits rustling, then walks in and kicks out the bird. Eli Spannagel, a rancher I used to work for in southeastern Montana, had a bassett hound that did much the same thing, except he didn't have to scrunch down much and when he got close to a rooster he bayed at it, which was quite effective.

My own two rough-shooting dogs have both been Labs, which is the safest way to go when bird work gets varied and unpredictable. The first was a very lean black dog with a white chest-blaze named Gillis. He didn't care for water (though he'd jump in and dive after wounded mallards) but really liked to insinuate his skinny body between rosebushes to scare the hell out of sharptails and pheasants. I toted it up once and in his almost fourteen-year existence he retrieved around twenty species of game birds, from doves to Canada geese, and a number of rabbits and hares. My present is a chocolate at the opposite end of the spectrum, a one-hundred-pounder named Keith who likes water as well as any pilot whale and prefers to go over pheasant cover rather than between it. In his first year I saw him slam head-on into several trees and fenceposts. He'd back up, look at them as if memorizing the exact diameter that had stopped him, then step aside and zoom onward. He has flushed everything from Huns (which he does rather well, quartering naturally in a grainfield) to a Shiras moose, which came out of our local pheasant cover late last season. Since I didn't shoot the moose, he didn't retrieve it, though if asked he would sure as hell try.

It may seem as if my experiences with rough-shooting dogs have tended toward flushers and off-breeds rather than pointing dogs. This is true, perhaps because pointing breeds have grown more specialized in the past couple of decades. This is, of course, because bird hunters have grown more specialized and stylized in the past couple of decades. A couple of seasons ago I took a friend up on his invitation to hunt his personal bird ranch. Upon arrival I found two huge pens full of pheasants, and soon learned that his private pheasant ranch is privately stocked. He ran German shorthairs, and looked a little askance at Keith. We worked several overgrown fields and some cattail creeks and, predictably, the pointers did better in the open cover and Keith did better in the cattails. At the end of the day my friend remarked that he could always put his pointers in a field worked by Labs or springers and find a few more birds.

I nodded and didn't say what I thought, which is that damn few of the pheasant places I hunt have roosters living in fields. Maybe on opening day, but after all the one-day wonders have worked the easy places, killing the easy birds, my pheasants seem to live in places a trifle more difficult than even overgrown fields. Cattails are one of the easier places, willow swamps being the hardest. My grouse tend to live in buffalo berry thickets or along alder-choked creeks. Doves and geese fly around fields, but the work is a little different than stylish pointing. I have known pointing dogs that did all these things, but not since Duchess have I seen one do all the rough stuff really well.

This is not to say that I don't enjoy walking a few 120-acre strips of wheat stubble behind a good English setter, talking to my friends and waiting for that classic point on a covey of Huns. This gets done, quite frequently. But the kind of bird hunting I do more often is a less stylized, more random. Despite early brainwashing by *The Old Man And The Boy*, my bird hunting has evolved into something much more akin to the Pleistocene than wearing a tie and standing around in groups watching several dogs work pen-raised birds. It has gotten so a great many bird hunters I know seem to expect similar experiences each time they go out. I listened to one such complain that he'd paid for four dozen quail for him and his three buddies, and they'd only gotten thirty-seven. This seems similar to what my father expected from the wild: a cost-effective hunt.

What Keith and I like to do is have adventures. My wife, Eileen, Keith's other alpha, says we get up in the morning like two goddamned chipmunks, tails wagging and looking forward to another day full of new scenery and unexpected thrills. We like to pick out a certain piece of Western landscape—willow bottom, durum wheat field, sagebrush, or ponderosa ridgetop—and go across it at a pace designed for nothing in particular. Like Duchess and all the other really good rough-shooting dogs I've ever known, Keith seems to be adapting to the terrain and bird rather than a gun club's notion of what an AKC Labrador retriever should be. When in willows, he circles the pheasants. When in sage, he snuffles the sage. When in wheat, he trots back and forth in front of me, nose higher and eyes alert. Wherever we go, we expect the unexpected, which is what dogs and men did a few millenia ago when they made their first looping travels along the unpredictable path of evolution. Perhaps that's the reason there aren't many rough-shooting dogs left these days; there aren't many rough-shooting hunters. Keith and I are regarded as recidivist mutations, which is just fine with us. There's more room out there for aimless drifters, and once in a while, past the fourth or fifth ridge, the sun falling at that four o'clock angle that makes every piece of buffalo berry or peachleaf willow or big sage seem ripe with expectancy, we even find a wild bird.

Chris Dorsey worked in Los Angeles as the senior editor of Petersen's Hunting *before becoming executive editor of* Ducks Unlimited. *He's the author of four books and his free-lance works have appeared in numerous national magazines including* Writer's Digest, Sports Afield, Field & Stream, Outdoor Life, Sporting Classics, *and a host of others. He's currently working on a book about waterfowling to be published by Lyons and Burford in 1995. He's a Wisconsin native who now lives in Memphis, Tennessee. He began training his first setter at the age of nine and has had at least one setter ever since—having a collection of chewed shoes to show for it.*

EXCLAMATION POINTS

by Chris Dorsey

Do we own bird dogs to hunt birds, or do we hunt birds to own bird dogs? A hunter's answer to that question tells much about him. Bird dogs can be both a curse and a blessing and any dog can transform from one to the other in a tail wag.

There is a kind of poetry, nevertheless, in watching a masterful pointer work the air currents, guided by the muses of the uplands. Indeed, in the recesses of every bird dog owner's mind dwells the perfect dog, a creature distantly related to the unicorn and the yeti. Perhaps it's our quest for that mythical dog that keeps us in rawhide chews and leather collars.

A great bird dog is more often defined by what it doesn't do than by what it does. I favor a consistent plodder over an occasional whizbang that's prone to fits of distant prospecting. No matter the dog work, though, a bird hunt without a dog is like a painting without a primary color, a drama without a protagonist, or a martini without an olive. For that reason, bird dogs are more than mere pets. To look at a bird dog as one would a guinea pig, hamster, or goldfish is to see no difference between a rabbit and a rabbit pellet.

There are many milestones in the life of a bird hunter but none that rival the purchase of a first pup. You don't care for a puppy as much as you give it a piece of your very being. When you invest wisely, the returns can be greater than any of Wallstreet's blue chips. A new pup is either a ray of sunlight that beams all the way to your heart or a shadow of mischief that can run off with your sense of humor. It is up to you to shape the course of your dog's life, for a pointer is an unbridled desire, a form of raw energy requiring harnessing to be useful.

The next memorable milestone in a bird hunter's life occurs when the pupil first locates a wild bird and comes to a staunch point. At that moment you don't know whether to flush and shoot the bird or fall to your knees, lift your hands to the firmament, and praise the Almighty.

Such a feeling came over me once when I acquired a dog after breaking a promise to myself to never accept another person's failed pup. "If you don't want her," said old Jack, the trainer who, after having put down more dogs than a Korean chef, had developed plenty of calluses on his conscience, "I'm going to have to get rid of her." That meant the next gunfire the year-old Irish setter would hear would be her last.

"I'll pick her up next week," I said, glancing at the lever-action .22 Jack kept in his pickup for the dogs that didn't measure up. I worked daily for most of the summer with Maggie and, though she showed some promise, she was as willful as any Irish lady. I had never worked with one of the red setters but had developed a sentimental kinship with the dog whose descendants probably confounded my ancestors every since my clan answered to the name O'Darcy on the Emerald Isle. I was once told of an Irish tale that explained the unruly behavior of a dog. As the yarn goes, dogs that misbehave do so because there's a tiny leprechaun hiding under their collars, whispering commands into the dogs' ears. By the end of the summer, I no longer wondered why the Irish had developed such an infatuation for whiskey. It wasn't the dreary climate nor a lack of spuds, it was their dogs. Then, one dew-soaked August morning, Maggie must have sensed my frustration. In what amounted to a canine epiphany, she snaked a course through the goldenrod, locating six wild pheasants in a series of points spaced no more than five

minutes apart. Her performance remains the most memorable single outing I've ever shared with a bird dog.

Despite such successes, rest assured that there will be setbacks on the trainer's journey. You'll likely discover, for instance, that bird dogs seem to have a particular fascination for skunks and porcupines—the same way young children can't resist writing with markers on a newly painted wall. Thor, the best dog I'd ever owned, winner of seven successive hunting dog trials, a dog that could reduce well-seasoned roosters to fricasseed pheasant with his mastery, could also locate a denned polecat anywhere on a section of head-high bluestem. If I saw a skunk dead on the road or so much as caught a faint waft of *essence de skunk* near an area I wanted to hunt, I'd load up and head elsewhere for fear the nearest town wouldn't have enough tomato juice to bathe the scent away.

Idiosyncracies aside, selecting a pup should be a matter of thoughtful consideration. Measure a dog's traits against its pedigree, the experts tell us, and carefully examine a pup's parents before making a decision in haste. Such advice, in most cases, is soon forgotten when a plump little pup wanders over and licks a prospective buyer on the chin. It's at that moment that people are especially prone to surrendering their wallet along with their common sense.

When it comes time to begin the process of molding your lump of canine clay, many people subscribe to the theory that old dogs will teach young dogs important skills critical to the success of a gun dog. I agree. My youngest setter, Frost, never knew how to dig tulip bulbs, chew door bottoms, and rearrange furniture until old Thor shared those invaluable lessons. I've often wondered if it wouldn't simply be easier to teach a pup to read a training book than to actually walk the student through the process myself. When you raise and train your own bird dog, you either share in the joy of having developed the prospect or suffer the pain of a plan gone awry. The outcome is never guaranteed, but nothing worthwhile comes without risk.

Too many modern dog handlers take the view that dog training is a testing of a dog's will against an electric collar, forgetting that the road to a finished bird dog is a scenic path traveled but once. The difference between a thoughtful approach to teaching and the work of an impatient trainer is the difference between taking time to smell the roses and simply mowing them. I've studied most of the so-called "new" methods of training bird dogs and, at the elemental level, they differ little from the advice given by old-timers decades ago. I suspect the methods haven't changed much because bird dogs and bird men haven't changed markedly over the years either.

We often romanticize that when our pointers are resting, their paws twitching in the depths of sleep, that they are dreaming of splendid days afield. In actuality, though, they're probably thinking of putting a choke collar on their owners and are wondering what it would be like if their trainers—albeit only for a moment—swallowed their whistles. Some of my most entertaining days in the uplands were spent watching otherwise sane men reduced to frothing idiots as they sprinted through cover in a desperate attempt to collar their runaway pointers—dogs seemingly deafened by an incessant chorus of whistle blasts.

One particularly lively hunt took place on a Wisconsin public hunting area—one of those places where 179 hunters and their dogs compete for the twenty roosters the state releases the day before the season opens. One of the birds—pheasants often referred to as "liberated" but about as free as an East German used to be to scale the Berlin Wall—flushed to face what amounted to a military maneuver. The bird fell instantly to one or more of the ten or twelve shots that rang out and, at the same moment, a half dozen dogs descended on it. A pointer reached the bird first and took two steps toward its master before being tackled by a yellow Lab. The Lab and the remnants of the pheasant were soon ambushed by a larger Lab and a setter and two German shorthairs joined the fray like a pack of famished wolves fighting over a lemming dinner. It was the last time I opened the Wisconsin pheasant season on a public hunting area.

I once thought I had owned some pretty rangy pointers until I attended my first field trial. I reasoned any dog that could outrun a horse was too much canine for me. My surmising was confirmed when I asked one of the trial men how many dogs he'd run at one time. He replied, "As many as I can afford to lose at one time."

No matter how well devised one's training techniques might be, frustration has a way of clouding even the most patient regimens. There isn't a dog trainer alive who, at least for a fleeting instant, hasn't wanted to strangle his dog with its ears. But I've seen as many dog owners as dogs who've needed an electric collar. We so commonly create a dog's fault and, in our haste to correct it, we too often make matters worse.

Given the precipitous peaks and expansive valleys of emotional terrain that accompany training a bird dog, prospective dog owners often ask me how long it takes to develop an effective pointing dog. The answer lies not in age but in experience—both the dog's and the trainer's. It's a matter of tabulating a dog's encounters with birds, for a young pointer with scores of introductions to birds will be more apt to cope with fowl than an older dog shy on exposure to game.

No amount of yard training can replace a dog's experience with birds. And a thousand pen-raised birds can't teach a dog the behavior of wild game. The difference between a pen-raised dupe and a wild bird is the difference between a birdbrain and a brain surgeon. That's a fact readily apparent with a pup's first hike into those magical places we call coverts. That's one reason I'm particularly fond of hunting with older dogs. Such veterans tend to use their wits more and their legs less. What the years take from them in speed they give back in savvy, and when you hunt with a sagacious pointer you never want for entertainment, for bird and dog are seldom long separated.

There have been reams of drivel devoted to the topic of which dog to use when hunting your favorite game bird. For instance, I've never owned a truly great ruffed grouse dog—at least not one that could consistently and stalwartly find and point grouse. But then, when it comes to hunting grouse, perhaps the most important trait a dog can possess is a sense of humor. The dog that can point grouse with regularity is, indeed, the four-leafed clover of the canine world. New England and the Great Lakes states are the hunting grounds of would-be grouse specialists that ended up woodcock general practitioners. Many mediocre pointers, in fact, owe their dog chow to timberdoodle.

When it comes to quail dogs, the best ones are the pointers that have never had their confidence shattered by the shenanigans of a sprinting pheasant. Who can blame a pheasant pointer for being a little neurotic and slightly hardmouthed? After desperately chasing a ringneck through marsh and meadow, a dog lucky enough to retrieve a rooster deserves a little revenge for its efforts. There's a fine line, however, between a little revenge and disemboweling a bird, a subtlety a friend's springer never quite mastered. If you didn't get to a fallen bird before the dog did, the best you could hope for was to have enough leftover for soup stock.

Perhaps you hunt your pheasants with one of the breeds termed "versatile" hunting dogs? I've been fascinated by this designation that's found a seemingly permanent place in the contemporary gun dog owner's lexicon. A versatile hunting dog, most often, is a moniker worn by any of the various pointing breeds originating from continental Europe. As a lifelong setter disciple, I've taken the term as a bit of an affront—sort of feeling the way I did when a Lutheran acquaintance used to refer to me as a mackerel snapper because of my Catholic heritage. I once owned a setter that could dizzy a pheasant with his wizardry, retrieved geese in ice water, and was rock staunch on raccoons. What's more versatile, I ask, than that?

Regardless of what breed of pointer graces your life, a good bird dog is the spice of any hunt in the uplands, adding a special flavor to the main course that is autumn. A bird dog is an interpreter of the air currents, relaying the story in the breeze through the cock of its ears or the wag of its tail. One is especially proud of his dog when those interpretations translate to more birds in the hand. Though I'm always appreciative of good dog work, I'm not prone to spoiling my setter, and I don't believe in feeding him scraps from the table. When he's fresh off a perfect performance, however, and has had a particularly keen day in front of both myself and friends, I'll set a place for him at the head of the table. No steak is too prime nor is any sofa too new for the bird dog that delivers close-flushing game to the gun.

Great bird dogs, too, are more than game finders. They're the alibis we need to flee our domesticated lives for a few moments of sanity in the marshes, fields, and woods. A good bird dog also travels well. That means he doesn't mind long sojourns in a pickup, and he knows how to peak around corners and run for the door when sneaking him into a roadside motel in bird country.

The spirit of a great dog, like the fire of a champion fighter, never quits. By the end of several consecutive days of hunting in Wisconsin grouse coverts, prickly ash and blackberry thorns would shred my setter's ears and scar his muzzle. He'd be one scab from nose to tail tip but, come the fifth day, no matter the temperature nor what hour of the morning I might awake, would greet me with the eager thump of his tail against the floor, ready to hunt again.

Most of all, a great dog never stops teaching its owner. And if an owner is wise, he'll never stop learning. A synchrony exists between an old dog and its owner, a synergy that builds with time spent together communicating in voice tones and body language. Birds might have first drawn us to the sport of wingshooting, but it's likely that our dogs have kept us in brush pants and double guns.

Bird dogs also introduce us to new friends, for gun dog owners often have much in common. My favorite bird hunting partners are people quick to notice even my setter's most remedial field successes and always offer a perfectly logical excuse when the dog appears a candidate for a lobotomy. Criticizing another's dog, on the other hand, has much in common with walking in a mine field, take one step too many and you may never come back.

No matter what our experiences with bird dogs have been, we will never forget them. Our memories of dogs past tend to age like fine wines. I even speak reverently about a friend's former hard-mouthed, deer-chasing, chicken-killing setter that used to hold a point until I was *almost* within shotgun range.

In spite of such regressions, is there a feeling so grand as sitting by a fire next to a tired bird dog that has hunted to exhaustion for you? To be certain, there is both a rhyme and a rhythm to hunting with a good gun dog. The melodic jingle of a dog's bell is the favorite tune of the upland gunner, for it reminds us of the age old question: Do we own dogs, or do they own us?

Dave Meisner is the publisher and editor-in-chief of The Pointing Dog Journal. *He's the founder and original publisher of* Gun Dog *magazine, which he sold in 1985. Dave and his wife, Barb, live in Des Moines, but Dave spends the bulk of his time pretending to be at work at his farmhouse-office on the edge of a 1,000 acre shooting preserve near Adel, IA. He is currently owned by a young Elhew pointer named Gilly, who is working hard to break Dave of fifty years of bad habits.*

IN THE HEART OF HER MASTER

by Dave Meisner

"Yes, sir, if you have never had a hunting dog, then you have missed out on a great part of life. It is as though you had been born without sight or hearing, or only half a heart. Once you have had a dog, you will have many more. Though some may hunt better than others, or do this and that, there will never be but one first dog. He will be with you always, in a special place, where no other dog or person can intrude. A little place which no one knows about and sometimes you are afraid to go there yourself because you cannot control the tears."

—Excerpted from "First Dog" in *Backtrack*
by Charlie Dickey

It's always cold in central Iowa in the middle of February, and it was especially so on this windy morning as I toiled in pre-dawn light. Still, a clammy sweat covered my forehead and glued my shirt to my back. I was in a sparse stand of timber and it had been difficult to clear even a small area of packed-tight frozen leaves, brush and branches, and especially to bust through two inches of frost with a pick axe in order to reach the softer dirt below.

It was not a good day, or a particularly good place to bury a dog...as if there could be either.

. . . . .

I bloomed late as a bird hunter, already married and in my twenties before I felt the urge to buy a hunting dog. I had started to read Hill and Evans and Spiller and Babcock and others who painted fascinating word pictures of bird dogs standing as stiff as brass cannons before proud masters. Somehow, for whatever reason, the till-then dormant hunter's gene within me awoke, and I found myself wanting to be in their stead.

The ad in the Green Bay paper simply read "English setter pups; $35. Call after 5:00." I had read that English setters were hunting dogs—what more mattered?

The next day Barb and I made the thirty-minute trip to Green Bay. We found the pups in an affluent neighborhood in the home of a dentist and his family. The dam was there and she was huge, with a massive head and floppy ears and jowls. She was white with orange ticking and she was, to be kind, *animated.* She yipped and panted and slobbered all over the good doctor's floors and furniture while he, oblivious to her lack of manners, showed us first one pup, then another. For what now are unfathomable reasons, we selected an active male who very much resembled his hyperactive mom. I offered $25; we settled on $30, and we headed home with my first "bird dog"...or so I thought.

I'd never owned nor attempted to train a dog before; I only knew what the books in my small collection told me, and the more I read—and experienced—the more I began to understand that Rusty, though a bird-dog breed, was definitely not a bird dog.

Rusty was from "show stock," the product of generations of breeding for looks and conformation, without regard for hunting ability. He had not an ounce of pointing instinct within him. Still, he was my dog, and in my blind and ignorant enthusiasm, I tackled the impossible task of making a bird dog out of him.

I took Rusty out frequently his first fall, and I'm sure we were quite a sight as we pushed aimlessly through the grouse woods near our home, a matched set: I had no idea what I was doing, and Rusty had no idea what I was trying to teach him to do.

I'd turn him loose and spend the next couple of hours totally frustrated as Rusty crashed through the woodlands, terrifying the creatures whose quiet domain we had invaded. He was a demon possessed, four-legged whirlwind—an orange belton Tasmanian devil!

When at last I would manage to collar him, Rusty showed no remorse, and no greater understanding of my pleadings than he had of my screamings. He'd just look at me quizzically, with his droopy, bloodshot eyes, and shake his head so drool from his big, sloppy jowls sprayed a half-dozen feet in either direction. He was a totally hopeless cause—living, breathing proof that breeding is more important than breed.

Eventually, I gave up and advertised Rusty "free to a good home," and though it was the last time I ever saw him, I didn't shed a tear when a local farmer packed him off to his new home in the country. I hoped Rusty lived happily ever after.

. . . . .

My search for a bird dog continued, and the next ad that caught my eye was in a Milwaukee paper. It hit hard on the one thing I had learned from my experience with Rusty: breeding is all-important. Just because a dog happens to be a bird dog breed, doesn't necessarily make it a bird dog. I had learned that, as a result of generations of breeding for conformation and the show ring, many pointing breeds simply don't point and won't hunt, just as many show-bred Labradors won't retrieve and can't swim.

Where Rusty would point nothing whatsoever, Samantha— at only eight weeks—pointed *everything*: meadow larks, grasshoppers, and frogs included. This pup, I quickly concluded, had the makings of a *real* bird dog.

Sam was a Brittany, and the dogs in her pedigree came from outstanding field-trial bloodlines. Her ancestors included, among others, Dual Ch. Pacolet's Sam, Dual Ch. Albedo Valley Dingo, Dual Ch. Pacolet's Cheyenne Sam, Dual Ch. Pontac's Dingo, Dual Ch. Tex of Richmond... a virtual "Who's Who" in the world of Brittany field trialing.

On exactly her forty-ninth day of life, Sam drove with me to her new home. She was to become "Mei-Stylish Samantha," and I thought that I had made the perfect choice in both breed and breeding. What I did not yet realize was that, while that breeding practically assured me of a dog possessed of great hunting desire and point, it also practically assured me of one with great range—a dog that would run, and run big... and how she did.

In 1971, at about Sam's first birthday, I packed up my family and we moved from our home in northeastern Wisconsin to bird-rich central Iowa. It was a career move, but one motivated in no small part by tales of Iowa's vast numbers of wild roosters and thirty-bird coveys of quail. Up to this point, I'd never shot a wild rooster—only the "put and take" variety—and I'd never so much as seen a quail except in books. I was not disappointed in Iowa.

In the early 1970s, even the public hunting areas near Des Moines held an abundance of birds, and Sam and I went after them with a primitive passion. Being new to Iowa, I hunted *alone*—and I do mean alone. Straight out of the dog box, Sam would head for the distant horizon to hunt birds; I hunted Sam. Most often the only clue I'd have as to her whereabouts was the distant cackling of flighted pheasants with a flash of white and orange in hot pursuit—oblivious to the screams and whistles of her would-be handler—shades of Rusty! But there were other scenes too, those that kept me coming back. In those early days especially, finding Sam locked on a quivering point was an adrenalin rush of monumental proportions.

She hooked me, and made a bird hunter out of me. Though I was frequently frustrated by her extreme range and uncontrollable desire to find birds, she gave me special moments that bonded us in a way only another dog-owning bird hunter can understand. We became the best kind of friends—forgiving of each other's faults—and the more we hunted together, the more I began to realize that it wasn't killing birds that mattered; it was the pursuit, and that undefinable element of "being there," but more, being there with my dog, with Sam. It was she who had addicted me to bird hunting, not the guns or the birds, or killing them. I knew after that first full season in Iowa that if I had to choose between hunting without a gun or hunting without my dog, the gun would lose, hands down, every time.

Sam was a big, old-school Brittany, with just enough of a mean streak in her to be a great watchdog. She didn't like kids, or people in general. Her world revolved around me. She slept at the foot of our bed and every night, right after I settled in, she'd walk over to my side and push her head under my hand. She had taught me that this action meant I was to scratch her head and ears, and it was she who would determine for how long. Some nights she might allow me this privilege for as long as two or three minutes before she'd pull away and retreat to the foot of the bed. Other nights, the scratching might last only twenty or thirty seconds—an obligatory scratch, if you will, because she needed to be consistent in her training of me. And she was; so far as I can remember, there was not a single night she did not initiate this ritual.

During our second year in Iowa, a new element was added to our now-favorite pastime—neighbor Norm Beattie was to become my close friend and constant hunting companion. Though dogless, he shared my enthusiasm for bird hunting, and he demonstrated his friendship in a profound way—in that he never, in a dozen years of hunting together, criticized my dogs. Such friends are hard to find.

We hunted often, and hard; we were intense students of the sport, becoming very good at what we did, and in Sam we had an efficient bird-finding machine.

Others will argue in favor of their dog, but I doubt the world has ever seen a dog that lived to hunt as much as Sam. When we'd turn off pavement onto gravel or dirt roads, she knew we were close to where we were going to hunt and she'd begin to claw at her crate and whine and howl, almost hysterically. There was nothing we could do to quiet her until at last we stopped and turned her loose.

There was nothing dainty or delicate about Sam. She barreled recklessly into the brushy draws of the farms we hunted, oblivious to multiflora rose and the piercing thorns of honey locust. It was rare that she wasn't bleeding from one place or another, or that something wasn't sticking in or out of her.

A Saturday morning in the mid-1970's found Norm, Sam, and me just north of the Missouri border on a day we shouldn't have been there. Though skies were bright, the real temperature was near zero and the wind chill was twenty below. I know better than to hunt quail on days like that now. On sub-zero days, quail need the warmth of a covey to survive. If a covey is busted by a predator—or a foolish hunter—the scattered singles may die of exposure before they can covey back up.

We hunted a few favorite draws without moving a bird. What had been slush the day before had fast-frozen into sharp and jagged ice floes that caused us to slip and Sam's pads to tear. Neither Norm nor I wanted to admit to each other how much we wanted to quit, while Sam seemed immune to the cold and was unrelenting in her search for birds. Blood from her pads splattered her underbelly and froze around her paws until it looked like she wore four red socks.

Norm and I seized Sam's bloody condition as our excuse to quit. We nearly raced back to my Bronco, loaded Sam into her crate, and turned the heater on full-blast—then lied to each other about how bad we felt about quitting as we jockeyed with the vents to send more heat our way.

Warm, welcome heat flowed into the Bronco as we pulled out of the farmyard onto gravel and headed home. We hadn't gone a quarter of a mile when, as luck would have it, Norm spotted a huge covey hunkered in a ditch beside the road. We drove 100 or 150 yards past it, stopped, got out, and quickly uncased and loaded guns. "There's no need for Sam," I told Norm, "her pads are too torn up—she's bleeding too bad—we can do this dogless."

That was my idea; Sam had others. As Norm and I started cautiously back in the direction of the birds, Sam began to howl and scratch at her crate like a wild animal caged for the very first time. She knew we'd spotted birds and she was having none of this stay-behind-and-wait-in-the-truck business.

Norm and I had already traveled thirty or forty yards down the road toward the tight-sitting covey before we concluded that we were kidding ourselves to think that Sam would let us do this alone. We knew from her desperate howls that she might kill herself, or at least do serious damage, if we didn't let her out and let her come along.

We hurried back to the truck and, after we opened her crate, she hit the ground with all four bloody feet flying. She'd waited long enough; now, there was no waiting for me and Norm. Full tilt and flat out, she made a perfect beeline in the direction of the unseen covey.

When she hit scent twenty yards from the birds, she was going too fast to do much about it. She tried to put on the brakes, but when she did, her legs slipped out from under her and she skidded on her side a half-dozen feet to the road edge, rolled once, and righted herself into a magnificent point. She stood like a statue with her head high and one leg up, blood forming a pool beneath it. It was an awesome sight!

By now the covey was understandably unnerved, and the thirty or more birds flushed just before Norm and I got into shooting range. Perhaps because of the extreme cold—and unlike a typical southern Iowa covey rise—the birds held tight together and sailed downhill, with us watching the entire flight, landing in a field of knee-high grasses. It was a quail hunter's dream come true; we knew exactly where they had landed.

We collared Sam, sat down, and waited. We knew where the birds were, but they were air-washed and we were looking for shots over points, so we waited for them to settle in, move a little, and give off some scent.

During the ten to fifteen minutes we strained to hold ourselves back, the blood flow from Sam's pads increased, and when we finally turned her loose, her red socks had turned to red britches. She was orange and white on top and red on the bottom, and in this quail shooter's eyes, beautiful, as she slashed downhill and through that grassy field, pointing one bird after another.

During the next half-hour, Norm and I took four birds each over points and missed as many, maybe a few more. It was below zero, but it might have been sixty degrees for all we knew. Sam pointed and held and retrieved, and pointed and held and retrieved, and kept doing it. Norm and I were imperfect that day; we shouldn't even have been there, but Sam was flawless, and of such hunts—though marred by our fallibility—are memories made.

· · · · ·

On July 15, 1974, I bred Sam to one of the winningest field trial Brittanys in the Midwest, Field Champion DeMadison King, owned by Walt Chapman of Des Moines, Iowa. Eight beautiful pups arrived sixty-three days later and I named the tailless bitch I kept "Lucky." She was not nearly as bold or aggressive as her mom—much more a lady, quieter, easier to train, more biddable. And while I admired the orneriness and aggressiveness of Sam, I knew I had something very special in Lucky. She was a lover, not a fighter, but she would have fought to the death for me, and she was a certain huntress, with the blood of generations of bird-finders coursing through her veins.

Lucky was loyal, both to me and to Sam, her mom. She was literally a trailer, following Sam wherever she went. She was most often the dog backing, seldom the dog on point, but it didn't matter to her—she accepted her role as second-string quarterback unquestioningly. Sam was the boss, period. And, this was true in our home—which they usually had the run of—in the kennel, in the yard, and in the field when we were hunting.

But while Sam was the leader of this two-dog pack, my allegiance slowly began to shift in Lucky's direction. Sam was my first real dog, to be sure, and nothing could ever change that. She was also a better bird-finder, had more desire, more stamina, better style, and more heart. But because of her enormous desire, Sam tended to self-hunt, not hunt for me. When I hunted Lucky with Sam, Lucky ran with Sam, but as I began to hunt her more and more often alone, she gradually developed into a very comfortable, medium-range shooting dog; hunting for me, not just with me or for herself.

As the years passed, the bond between me and both dogs grew. Each was special to me in her own way. And, as my knowledge of bird dogs increased, and I came to more fully understand the role of a class bird dog, I was finally able to appreciate Sam's range and desire. Seeing her cutting an edge a half-mile to the front no longer bothered me, but instead, brought a smile, and even goose bumps.

While I admired Sam's special qualities and loved to watch her bust the horizons of the pheasant and quail country we hunted in central and southern Iowa, I turned to Lucky when I needed a reliable and steady shooting dog. It was she alone who went with Norm and me to our grouse and woodcock coverts in northeast Iowa; she who shared a sleeping bag with me on one particularly cold night in Yellow River State Forest when it was still primitive. The real temperature dropped to ten below that night, and the only heat we had in our tent was a Coleman lantern.

The next day the temperature rose to an almost-warm twenty above; the sun was shining and the skies were blue, as Norm, Lucky, and I strolled beautiful snow-covered logging roads through a soundless woodland.

That morning we experienced a sight most grouse gunners have read about, but only the fortunate have experienced. The night before—to escape from the bitter cold—a grouse had burrowed deep into the soft snow in the middle of the trail that now lay before us. I'll always remember the fantastic explosion of white as the grouse blasted out not a dozen feet in front of us, scaring two grown men and a now-experienced bird dog half to death.

He went my way, and I recovered from the shock of his exit just in time to shoulder a little 20-gauge, punch the trigger, and watch the bird fold. Lucky made a fine retrieve across the glistening white landscape, and the three of us sat for a long time, wishing we had it all to do over again.

· · · · ·

I live today with many memories of days afield with those two dogs, almost all good memories, because—as it should be—the bad ones have faded into obscurity.

Sam and Lucky were my constant companions, not just during the bird season, but all year long. They were well-trained and listened to me, and that, in part, is why it's so very hard to explain what happened to them.

In early 1980, we lived in a home well out in the country, at the end of a nearly mile-long gravel road. There was a lot of wildlife in the area, including deer. A fateful February afternoon Barb returned home from taking both dogs to the vet. She opened the station wagon doors and released them each from their crates. The slamming of the tailgate spooked a doe standing at the edge of the woods not far away, and both dogs took off in reckless pursuit, Lucky on Sam's heels, as usual. They didn't come back that night.

This dilemma was complicated by that fact that I was scheduled to go out of town on business the next day and Barb was going with me. This meant no one would be around our home when and if the dogs came back. It was impossible to cancel the trip, so I did the only thing I could do—I notified the closest neighbors, our vet, and the local sheriff's department, asking all of them to keep an eye out for the dogs while we were gone. Of course, we never had any way of knowing whether they returned to the house or not during the three days and two nights that we were gone. I strongly suspect they did, and had we been there, I believe this story would have a different ending.

I searched hard for the dogs after we got back from our trip, spending many anxious hours driving what seemed like hundreds of miles on the county trunks and gravel roads around our home. I had everyone I knew looking, and I posted notices in the convenience stores and gas stations in the area.

At midnight, eight days after their disappearance, the phone rang. It was the voice of a young man.

"Sir, on my way home from work tonight I spotted a dead dog lying on the side of the road. It was an orange and white dog. I took its collar off; I have it with me, and it has your name and number on it."

Barb was watching me, hoping the call was good news. She knew it wasn't as I fought to respond to the caller through the growing lump in my throat.

"The dog's name is on the collar," I said, "Tell me what it is, please."

"Sam."

I swallowed hard as my lips tightened and eyes glazed. Barb looked at me and asked in a whisper, "Which one?"

"Sam is dead," I answered. She lowered her head and left the room so I wouldn't see her tears.

The caller was patient and understanding, and waited through a long and awkward pause for my next question. "I lost two dogs," I finally continued, "did you see another one in the area?"

"No."

Knowing that I had lost Sam was heartbreaking, but now finding Lucky took precedence over all else.

"How do I get to your house? I'd like to have the collar back, I want to pick up my dog to bring her back here to bury her, and I have to look for my other dog."

"Come to my house first; I'll give you the collar and I'll sketch out a map that will show you how to find your dog."

He gave me his address, which was in a small town a few miles from where the dogs had run off. When I got there he was courteous and sympathetic, gave me the collar and the map, and assured me again that he'd seen only one dog.

As I drove alone to the spot on the map—a desolate stretch of a county trunk—a horribly strange mixed emotion tormented me. I was in a hurry to get there because I wanted to find Lucky, but at the same time I dreaded getting there, because I knew I'd find Sam.

The outer glow of the headlights fell on her, and I eased the car onto the shoulder of the road. And then, I saw the other form—not ten feet away. To my horror, there was not one dead dog, but two. I couldn't move; I just sat there—stunned, motionless—with my mouth open and my eyes fixed in a helpless glaze.

I wondered at first how the caller could have missed two dogs that close together, but then, when I finally approached Lucky and touched her lifeless form, the awful suspicion that had raced through my numbing mind was confirmed: She was still warm, and the blood that trickled from her nose and mouth was still moist; Lucky had been hit only a short time before I got there. I sat on the cold road surface, with Lucky cradled in my arms, and cried.

I will never know, this side of eternity, what happened that terribly sad night, but knowing both dogs as I did, I can speculate. Sam was probably killed early on, perhaps the first night or two; otherwise, she would have come home. I suspect Lucky, because of her fierce loyalty to Sam, refused to leave her body— staying instead for those many days and nights to guard it from the monster cars and trucks that infrequently roared past. I see her to this day, in my mind's eye, spending the endless hours standing vigilantly at her mom's side, boldly and protectively, yet scared, and surely confused. Sam had always been there with her, every day of her life. How could Lucky understand the cold stare in the old dog's eyes and the unresponsiveness of death?

When the caller drove by, perhaps Lucky was off foraging for food, or perhaps she was hunkered in a nearby ditch. If only I had traveled that stretch of road during the hours I searched, if only the caller had spotted her a day earlier—an hour earlier. If only…

. . . . .

No, it was not a particularly good day—that cold, February morning in 1980—to bury a dog…or two. But I know now, a dozen plus years later, that I buried them in the right place. I learned of it from Ben Hur Lampman and his famous essay, "Where to Bury a Dog." After considering numerous plausible burial sites, Lampman sagely concludes that there is but one best place to bury a dog, and that is in the heart of its master.

There now reside Sam and Lucky.

As George Bird Evans wrote in *The Bird Dog Book*, "The death of a dog is the price of a priceless experience, having had them."

And so it was.

Datus Proper says he was born in Iowa, raised in Montana, domesticated at schools in New Hampshire, New York, and New Mexico. He survived employment in Angola, Brazil, Ireland, Portugal, and Foggy Bottom, D.C. Datus invariably preferred hunting and fishing to the alternative, such as working and claims to have been run out of every town within four years. He lives today on the banks of a spring creek in the Gallatin Valley of Montana, surrounded by schools of trout, wisps of snipe, sords of mallards, and nides of pheasants.

LANGUAGE LESSONS

by Datus Proper

Jim McCue is partly to blame for what happened, mind you. When I was looking for a pup with the right ancestors, Jim's dog was winning the biggest field trials for German shorthaired pointers, so naturally I inquired about the champion's social life. Jim told me of a promising litter and I bought Huckleberry over the telephone—one of the quickest of life's big decisions. Jim and I met a few days later at an abandoned airport, turned the pup loose, and watched him try to catch a flock of starlings before they gained altitude. Jim said that I should let the pup tear around like that for his first year, building up enthusiasm. By the time Jim finished his sentence, Huck was out of sight and I was wondering how much more enthusiasm to expect.

Back home, I introduced the pup to a brand new kennel and concrete run—built for my wife, in a sense, because she had run out of enthusiasm for dogs that dribbled on her floors. It turned out that I should have used a thicker door for the kennel. Huck clawed a hole in the plywood and Anna thought he looked cute, peeking out for company, so she allowed him in the kitchen while I was armor-plating his quarters. By the time I was done, Anna remarked that the pup did not drool. A couple of hours later she reported that he had housebroken himself. After some few months, I sneaked out of my office and heard Huck telling Anna a tale that was making her giggle. His pronunciation was weak, you understand, especially on the consonants. What caught my attention was that he was imitating the cadence of my wife's speech and the pitch of her voice. Must have been a funny story, too, because she's Irish, with more feeling for tragedy than comedy. I'd never realized that she had such a pretty laugh.

Languages are easy to learn, at the right time of life, and that time—for humans—is before puberty. Little children can learn even Irish Gaelic, which is more than I have managed. The right timing turns out to be crucial, however. Neuropsychologists now believe that early childhood is a "critical period"—the time during which a human *must* be exposed to his or her mother tongue. A child that fails to acquire language skills does not develop the necessary brain circuits and is impaired for life. Work is being done on critical periods in dogs, too, and it is going to change the ways we raise puppies. Meanwhile, most of us have probably known dogs with circuits missing.

I do not mean to push the analogy. Huckleberry is a communicator, but neither his logic system nor his sound system has evolved in the same way as mine. What he thinks is language is, in fact, just a game. On the other hand, puppy games made him a faster learner than the kennel-raised dogs I've worked with. In particular, the way he picked up trailing seemed unusual, for a pointing dog.

During that first fall, Jim McCue's advice gave me the excuse to do what Huck and I both wanted anyhow, which was to run wild. There were bigger things than puppy training for me to worry about just then. I needed an optimistic little bundle of energy to exorcise my emotions, focus them at infinity. Optimism was part of Huck's personalities—both of them. "House angel, field demon," Anna called him. When Huck glimpsed our pond for the first time, he took a flying leap into it and

swam toward my wife, who thought he was drowning. "My puppy!" she screamed. I had not heard that tone in her voice since our baby rolled down the stairs (with similar results). Anna waded in to save Huck. He climbed out on his own, shook water all over her, then jumped back in and swam across the pond to me.

A pup this bold would not have been daunted by more early training in obedience. On the other hand, I do not regret my failure to train Huck on the usual tame bobwhites and pigeons. In lieu of them he pointed the meadowlarks, flustered the ducks, and chased the magpies. It might not have been everyone's idea of fun but the most important thing in matching man and dog, I suppose, is temperament. Part of me was right out there running with the pup, eyes shining, tongue hanging out.

The first pheasant that Huck pointed was a hen, which I of course flushed with fanfare. There were not many cocks around but he started pointing those he ran into. I took the finds as serendipitous—gifts from the angels. Any pup can run into a bird, and a pup of the right breeding is always going to point strong scent. It's in his genes. You don't know that you've got a real pheasant dog till he learns trailing.

When Huck was six months and eleven days old, however, my enthusiasm and his reached the same level. He started trailing in grass that was, I thought, too low for a pheasant. I watched for a while, concluded that he was doing a good job of hunting the wrong thing, and decided to ignore him. Hiked fifty yards. Realized that I was alone, looked around, and saw the pup on point. Ran back, caught the bird between us, waited out a great noisy glittering flush, and dropped a rooster in plain sight. Huck pounced and retrieved. He had done it all, seen it all, made the connection.

Two days later, almost at dark, he went on point in cattails. I tried extra-hard to shoot well, which is of course the best way to miss, and the rooster came down winged. I saw it land in a patch of brush and heeled Huck to the place. He tore off across an open field. I kept whistling him back, making him hunt the brush. The stars came out. We did not find the bird till the next day, by which time it was bones and pretty feathers, the rest eaten by a skunk. The bird had in fact headed across the open field and Huck had been on its track, if only I had let him follow his nose. That was the last time I tried to teach him anything about trailing.

In his second season, when the pup was a year old, he lost none of the hundred-odd birds that my friends and I shot over him. Hardest to smell were the singles of gray (Hungarian) partridges. Members of the grouse family ran as well as the partridges but left more scent. Pheasants, of course, were the long-distance champions, covering up to a measured mile. It seemed, too, that they shared some of the partridges' ability to suppress scent in an emergency.

Huck was experienced, considering his tender age, but he was not trained by the usual field-trial rules. He remained free to creep or break point in order to stay with a moving bird. Perhaps some pups can trail as well as Huck without being allowed equal discretion. I just haven't seen them.

A year-old pup on his own discretion was, of course, often indiscreet. He would stand on point as long as his bird held, but when it moved there were various possibilities. Hardest of them to handle was a maneuver we'll call the Montana Sprinting Squat. Pickup drivers have a similar ploy called the Texas Rolling Stop, during which the truck coasts through an octagonal sign at forty-five miles per hour. You are supposed to take good intentions into account. Pheasants intend to flush but not within eleven inches of a dog's nose, so they sprint till achieving the velocity of a Texas Rolling Stop and then go airborne, total elapsed time 0.7 seconds.

Fortunately, the Montana Sprinting Squat always worked and the birds always escaped. They were wild and strong, remember. You could not let a pup chase pen-raised birds or he'd catch some of them and perhaps decide that he could hunt successfully on his own. Huck learned that he only got pheasants when we worked together. I ladled on praise when he did things right, of course, but a bird in the mouth was all the encouragement he really needed. At the end of a day we'd both tell my wife that we'd had fun but it was not fun, exactly. It was the happiness that comes with pheasant feathers.

My system (or nonsystem) might be wrong for you. You might lack wild birds or the time to work a pup on them. Your wife might not provide language lessons for the youngster. You might have a kennel-raised dog, or one with less point in his genes. Your specialty might be eastern ruffed grouse, in which case you would be wise to insist that your dog point at first suspicion of scent and hold till released. For covey birds like the partridges and quails, I'd have preferred Huck steady to wing and shot, too, because a dog that breaks can spoil a covey rise. But for the rest I wanted him to trail. I wanted him to get me shots at the old cocks that considered themselves immortal. I wanted him to find winged birds no matter how far they ran. The rewards seemed worth the risk.

A "dog that's going to be any good puts his nose where the scent is," high or low. That's what William Harnden Foster wrote about grouse dogs back in 1942, and Huckleberry reached the same conclusion. When air scent failed, he would work a patch of snowberries on ground scent till I called him off, and a cock would flush the moment my back was turned. It turns out that roosters can run around for a long time in the same half-acre of brush. You might not want to waste time on such birds—if you have easier hunting available. We did not.

Working air scent, on the other hand, was anything but tedious. The pup would trail from one end to another of a two-hundred-acre field of grasses planted under the Conservation Reserve Program. Or he'd follow birds out of a brushy bottom, up weedy draws, and into wheat stubble. Some of the pheasants would hold tight at the end of the trails. Others would flush wild. It's what most owners of pointing dogs would have pre-dicted, and what some would call disaster. The pheasants cer-tainly considered it disaster, because we got our share at the end of the trails. I earned the shots, mind you. My wife was teaching aerobic dance classes, working out on a ski machine, and watching her calories while I was eating like a sumo wrestler and getting skinnier by the week. Huck was going through ten cups a day of the expensive high-fat dog food. If you don't want exercise, stay away from pointer pups bred for all-age field trials.

When you run a young dog almost every day, something happens to its body as well as its mind. Huck put on ten or fifteen pounds of muscles that he would not have developed if he had spent his youth in a kennel. The weight was in the right places, because running is complete exercise for a dog. Being light-boned, he did not look heavy. His brown hair was shiny as a seal's. His pads gave no trouble. His pace would have exhausted any other dog I've had in two days, but Huck kept it up all season. There was, however, a disadvantage that I learned when partridge season opened the next year on September 1: muscles hold heat. I had to whistle him in frequently, sit him down in shade, and give him water. When duck season came, swimming was harder for him too, because his body was so dense that he had to work just to stay afloat. A serious water dog needs some fat.

Perhaps trailing, the way Huck does it, really is a skill that must be acquired before puberty. I don't know. At various times, however, I have watched him hunt with seven other pointing dogs, and that's counting only the good ones. Some of the seven are competitive with him in shoot-to-retrieve trials; one is his half brother. All can follow hot body scent. When Huck takes off after a really sneaky rooster, however, the other dogs have learned that the only way to get involved is to run loops in front of him. That maneuver takes brains, too, of course.

I watch the other dogs when the realize that Huck is on a tough trail. They deduce what is going on but cannot get the hang of it themselves. They look at him as if he were speaking Gaelic, sort of.

Diane Vasey says her life went to the dogs by the time she was twelve, when she started taking her family's cocker spaniel to obedience classes. She spent the next two decades learning all she could about every hobby related to canines. Today, she is editor-in-chief of the AKC Gazette *magazine for purebred dogs, and lives in Connecticut with her Lab, champion papillons, and cocker spaniels. Former editor of* The Pointing Dog Journal, *she has participated in field trials with her pointers, enjoys quail and waterfowl hunting—and trout fishing at every opportunity. A conscientious breeder, she says there are few things more fun than raising young puppies—but one pleasure that offers immense satisfaction is being able to see a pup grow to reach his potential and become all he was meant to be.*

GILLY

by Diane Vasey

To one who has seen many, there are dogs and then there are *dogs.*

A person who is seasoned in the business of dogs, one who has flirted with the fancy long enough to have seen fashionable breeding and training trends become historical lessons of genetic or environmental dysfunction, assumes a sort of circumspective attitude when an enthusiastic neophyte seeks his opinion about a dog or puppy. He responds to such inquiry with casual and vague generalities that are virtually meaningless to the approval-seeking questioner.

To the would-be field trialer with a puppy entry: "Got some fire, doesn't he?"

To the hunt-test enthusiast with a versatile breed: "Thorough little guy, isn't he?"

To the conformation show hopeful: "That pup looks real *nice* right now."

Nice? And the uninitiated walk away without a clue about what they have or what the enlightened really thought of their prospect.

Why does one with expertise respond with such vagaries? Because he knows. The veteran fancier developed this attitude over time, obtaining wisdom from hard-earned firsthand experience. He knows that every prospect may become the "dream" dog for the guy at the other end of the leash, but that most never will achieve their potential—and that, of those who do, most will merely blend with the multitudes, having some good qualities and some weaknesses, the sum of which keeps them from standing out in the crowd.

So it is that most dogs come into our lives and then go, without notorious fanfare. They do what we ask of them while we provide their needs, their contributions ultimately well worth the effort it takes to keep them well and happy. Whether good or bad, they steal our hearts, and we are hooked for life (theirs). When they go, we mourn their departure and they linger in our memories for a time, fading eventually into blurred, shadowy images biased by time and selective retention.

On rare occasion, though, we encounter an exceptional being, one whose uncanny abilities raise the possibility of the purported sixth sense—a mystery that imparts an almost eerie feeling of wonder and awe in those who are fortunate to know the animal beyond casual acquaintance. This is the dog, just one in a multitude, who transcends our common understanding of the species, one whom we ineptly describe as "almost human."

If the dog who possesses this level of intelligence also possesses physical qualities for capable athletic performance, and if the dog ends up with an owner who recognizes potential and has the skills and resources to develop it, we have, in effect, a dog to die for. We have the stuff of which legends are made.

Such was the case with Gilly, a pointer prodigy I had the fortune to raise this past fall—a serendipitous, all-too-brief experience for which I can accept little credit.

I had been editor of *The Pointing Dog Journal* magazine for about a year when I had an opportunity to get a pup that seemed to fulfill all of my rather lengthy prerequisites for adoption. The publisher of the magazine, Dave Meisner, was interested in participating in the development of and in sponsoring a pup for different types of events and competitions. He agreed that my future pup could come to the office each day, and he looked forward to the training ventures that would become a part of the office environment.

Because selection of the line and the breeder of a pup is much more critical than actually choosing the individual, I spent an inordinate amount of time considering characteristics and abilities of generations of producers. I finally settled on the credits and reputation of Bob Wehle, a man who had been breeding pointers for fifty-seven years. His dogs had been bred for function and form, which would contribute to intelligence, biddability, and class. Elhew Kennels had produced gun dogs for bird hunters and field trial dogs that had won every type of competition imaginable, and had done so consistently throughout decades. Arrangements were cinched after Dave and I talked with Bob himself; we were pleased to discover that he truly fit his reputation as a stalwart believer in evaluating the total dog before breeding it, one who will sacrifice an outstanding inheritable trait if the dog should not be bred because of a bad inheritable flaw, a conscientious man of sound principle— and a gentleman's gentleman.

Despite months of homework and careful deliberation, however, I was not prepared for what I saw when I picked up the pup at the Chicago airport. Bob's description of the pup had been accurate: He was orange-and-white, symmetrically marked with a black nose and black eyeliner. But more important, Bob also had said that the pup was special, his pick puppy in an outstanding litter that he planned to keep himself.

From the moment he stepped out of his crate, the little pup carried himself with an air of nobility. A dignified puppy is oxymoronic—yet if the concept were possible, this puppy would have been dignified. His aura was subtle and is hard to describe, and perhaps only a connoisseur of canines would even have noticed—but I sensed it within ten minutes after letting him out of the crate to potty.

This 10-week-old pointer stepped into grass near the office, blinked, yawned, blinked again, took a quick survey of the scene while he relieved himself, saw me and made a beeline. When he reached me, he tugged my ruffled ponytail hairpiece from its place, flipped it into the air and then stalked it, freezing into a picture-perfect, classic, poker-straight high-tailed point. Dave and I looked at each other and I saw wonder in his eyes.

"Sheeesh," he said. "Wow; Diane—that dog is incredible."

We tossed the hairpiece and played the game repeatedly with similar results. Smiling, I scooped up the puppy, and Dave and I looked at each other and shook our heads.

"This is gonna be fun."

. . . . .

The next six months were filled with a mixture of joy and heartache.

He was named Elhew's Upland Gilly, after the hunting and fishing guides of the Scottish Highlands.

Gil went along everywhere I could take a dog, and some places where they normally were not allowed. At about twelve weeks old, he went along with magazine staff on a press check to St. Croix Press near Minneapolis. Employees were intrigued when they heard there was a pointer puppy in the CEO's office. They wanted to see him point. We didn't have a rod-and-wing handy, so we improvised with what was available in the office. Those who came in to see him spread the word after they left, and by late afternoon there had been a steady stream of visitors who had come to see him do his stuff. He was a predictably consistent and reliable performer. When people came, we would pull out a white tissue and snap it to the end of a leash. We tossed it to the floor and he would transform into a statue— no, a sculpture—of a bird dog on a classic point, tail straight to the ceiling. And he would remain on point until the tissue was flipped out of sight and hidden. At one time, there were about a dozen people standing in the room talking and watching him.

They would come in, marvel, and leave, but through all the commotion, he never acknowledged anything except the tissue for as long as it remained on the floor.

Truth is, when the Good Lord passed out personality, Gilly must have been first in line. He was full of it, and full of himself, and he burst with it in all he did.

Gilly's puppyhood was riddled with mischief and adventure. When some kids took their sleds to a snowy hillside, he perceived it as an opportunity to create games the kids had never played. He would start down the hill chasing the kids and wind up sliding, like an otter, his mouth wide open and tongue lolling out the side. Once at the bottom, he figured it must be a race to the top, and he'd win the race if he could pull the kids down on his way. When the kids threw snow to retaliate, he would leap to catch all he could.

He loved "happy time" on the soft couch, where he would tunnel between the cushions and flip upside down, burying his head and snorting. It was on the couch that he learned to love being rubbed all over, and to this day he greets people he likes with a catlike rub against their legs.

When faced with a canine dilemma, he would cock his head in thought, assessing the situation and devising a plan for solution or disaster—whichever came first.

When he wanted something out of his reach on the kitchen counter, he would figure out an alternative route to get it— even if it meant starting at the other end of the kitchen and using the trash can to climb up, walk across the range top, around the microwave, over the sink, and past the toaster to get to his destination.

I don't think Gilly was born with all of that problem-solving braininess, though—I think he got some of his smarts and much of his rebelliousness from watching too much television. He liked to lay on the couch or sit in front of the TV and watch the Discovery channel. I know he preferred that channel to MTV because he would stand up with his ears perked forward every time birds flew across the screen, as if waiting for them to fly out of tube into the family room.

One thing he did not like was bears, and if a grizzly showed up on the screen, he would get up and walk stiff-legged, with hair on end, to peer behind the TV. I think he wanted to make sure that no bears would sneak out the TV's back door to join us.

His all-time favorite late-night viewing was when I would pop popcorn ("one for you, three for me"), start a bird-dog training video produced by his breeder, and invite him to curl up on the couch. There was no doubt in anyone's mind that he recognized Bob Wehle and the familiar bobwhite whistle that Bob uses in early training. Gil would stand up and freeze, like he was honoring the dog in the video. After the birds flew, he would get excited and paw me, as if asking me to rewind it!

. . . . .

Life seemed grand at the time to both of us, he without a care in the world and me with grandiose plans for shared trips afield and in hunt tests and field trials. We lived in blissful ignorance of the events that would change our lives and signify the end of our time together.

When the publisher of *The Pointing Dog Journal* first told me he was considering selling a part of the ownership of the magazine to other investors, I was not concerned for the welfare of the magazine or my position as editor. We had thousands of devoted subscribers; we had won the highest quality award and recognition possible to us in 1993 from the Dog Writers Association of America; and our first set of renewals had just started to come in. The wind shifted for me personally, however, when greed bungled the first investor's offer and the deal fell apart. A second investor, a publishing company complete with its own several magazines and existing editorial and production staff, became interested in the *Journal.* A merger took place shortly thereafter. Soon I was trying to decide the direction to take for the rest of my career: editing for a different employer, becoming self-employed as a publisher or freelance writer, or going back to school.

Eventually I opted for returning to school to pursue becoming a veterinarian. My biggest challenge, I thought, would be figuring out how to do that without giving up my pointer, Labrador retriever, cocker spaniel, and papillon. I had grown accustomed to owning a home, and renting is problematic when you have dogs. Tuition money was a problem, too, I found, because federal loans were not available to "special students," or people who already had a master's degree. To save every penny I could, I hoped to find a place that would not charge rent, or charge as little as possible, in exchange for some kind of service I could offer—perhaps assistance for an elderly person.

It was tough. I had offers that would take me without the dogs, or with just one small dog. But no one really wanted to deal with a growing pointer puppy. It was beginning to look like I would need a miracle. That's how we came to live with the Doneffs.

Nick and Kris Doneff are a good Christian couple who took pity on me and offered to put a roof over my head until I found something else. They thought that having Gilly temporarily might be fun for their kids, who were ten and twelve. They also had two toy poodles and two cockatiels, but we had it all figured out: The Lab would stay temporarily with a friend in Missouri who hunts waterfowl, and he would get a litter out of her in return; the cocker would stay with another friend in Wisconsin, and they would get a puppy in return; and the papillon and Gilly could stay at the Doneffs.

Problem was, no one knew what to expect from the Gil Monster. All I could do was cross my fingers and hope for the best. Things seemed to start out okay, but...

Gilly kept on growing. As his muscles developed, he became more coordinated and athletic. He began to show us what a true, powerful, gutsy bird dog should be made of—and it wasn't sugar and spice. I have to admit that I was awed by his prowess— I had seen a lot of bird dogs grow up, but this one never stopped surprising me. Unfortunately, I seemed to be alone in true appreciation of his physical capabilities. One day his impressive agility led to his exile.

I had just brought him in from a romp outside, which was intended to burn off pent-up energy that had earlier caused him to accumulate a series of not-so-delicate etiquette-related offenses. We were headed through the house toward my bedroom when he decided to take a shortcut. Suddenly, he leapt over the couch without touching it, landed on the other side, and launched himself onto the table beyond, scattering papers and such in all directions. Quite pleased with his new Olympian feat, he looked down from the table at the Doneff's two toy poodles, who were now barking at him from below, glanced over at me, and grinned.

It was an ill-fated circumstance that, at that precise moment, Kris happened to walk into the room. Her eyes widened as she stopped and stared at our Pegasus, and I quickly tried to reassure her.

"This, too, will pass." I smiled weakly.

"Yes," she said, ever so politely, stifling a laugh (lest, perhaps, Gil be encouraged?). "Of course. When do you think it'll pass?"

I looked at Gil, still obviously pleased with himself, and I knew that my answer would have significant ramifications for his being welcome in the house. Mustering all the credibility of an expert in canine development, I said, "Well, you know, these hunting dogs are bred to be athletes. We expect them to have the physical ability to leap over rivers and cross mountains in pursuit of birds."

"I see."

"Yeah, and then we expect them to come into the house and lie quietly at our feet, causing no disruption, and basically just snooze away time."

"Uh huh."

"Well, you know, it takes time to teach them that..." I seemed to be losing ground.

"Hmm."

I looked back at Gilly, who wriggled with pleasure, wagged a high tail, and appeared to be challenging me to a game of King-of-the-Mountain from the tabletop.

"Okay, okay, " I said, resigning myself to straight-from-the-shoulder candidness: "In about two or three years, he'll be so calm in the house, you wouldn't know he was the same dog."

"Really."

So it was that the Gil Monster received "time-out" in the kennel without parole, to think about his manners. To his misfortune, it happened to be the coldest Wisconsin winter in twenty-five years, and no one in the family wanted to live outside in the doghouse with him. I felt bad about his new quarters, but reminded him that he had brought it upon himself, and that he was lucky they were letting me run electricity out to the dog-house for heat.

He accepted his lot without complaint, and I tried to make up for it by increasing our time afield. Our daily romps out back through the woods and fields grew longer as he grew stronger. Often the snow was deep and he would bound through it like a jackrabbit, his ears flying as he appeared and disappeared with each leap.

Like no other dog I've seen, Gil had a spirit of profuse and unfettered joy. Unrestrained as it was, his exuberance was contagious, and it was on these walks that I felt my spirit mesh with his, lifting ever higher, and I thrilled to it vicariously. When the snow melted, he would sail past with gazelle-like grace, seeming to float effortlessly back and forth ahead of me, savoring through his nostrils all that the earth had to offer.

Watching him get into birds would raise goose bumps on the arms of an honest dog man. Catching scent, Gilly would pivot midair to land on point, with style that would make your blood race nearly as fast as his. He would quiver with controlled eagerness, as if every muscle was in tetany, overdosed for the flush. He was rigid on the tips of his toes, mesmerized by the irresistible fragrance that teased his nose and stirred his hair to its end. He was at once both inebriated and impassioned; and when the birds flew, he was so deeply entranced that at first he could not move—then he seemed to regain consciousness, collect himself and charge for all he was worth after the birds, sure that he would sprout wings and soar until he caught them.

With Gilly, nothing was ordinary or mundane. To him, every-thing was recklessly fun and fascinating, and he experienced life in a venturous frame of mind that was fueled by a super-charged engine. You could not walk with this dog and watch him run without smiling and feeling yourself come alive too.

But as the days and weeks went by, school became more demanding, my time became more limited, and our walks became shorter and less frequent. The commute to school was an hour and a half each way; classes sometimes went from morning till night, and some nights I could not make it home at all.

On those nights, the Doneffs took care of Gilly's needs. I encouraged the kids to let him out of the kennel for play, but I knew he needed more structured exercise and training. He was far too intelligent to spend hour upon hour in a kennel, and I became concerned that boredom would make dull his mind and limit his development—or worse, lead to behavior problems.

Had he been less intelligent, less physically capable, or less—humanlike, I might have been able to invent creative ways to ensure his well-being without feeling that my absence was depriving him of reaching his potential. But his was such a rare combination of ability and intelligence that I knew he would be better off with someone who had the time and resources to help him develop into all that he could be.

I believed that keeping Gil from attaining his potential could be likened to keeping Beethoven from developing and composing a symphony. Gil had the potential to become a bird dog exemplar, but if I did not have the time or resources to direct his growth, he would not ever become the artisan that Beethoven was—he would never make fine music.

I knew, too, that my motives for keeping him were selfish. But selfish motives are strong ones. At a time in my life that was riddled with hardship and stress, he was my joy—my freedom. He was my relief from all that was painful, and I loved him.

Because I loved him, I could not bring myself to let him go to someone else; I knew that I would never have another like him. But because I could not give him the time he needed and deserved, I was hurting him. Both options had bleak consequences; I was torn between selfish desire and selfless devotion.

Then one day I returned to him after a two-day bout at school and I thought he had lost weight. I checked his self-feeder. It was full of food, but the magnetic swinging door on the side of the feeder, which was designed to keep the food dry but allow the dog to eat when he pushes against it, was in its closed position. I had been propping it open because Gil, never a hearty eater, would rather not eat than push against the door to feed. I suspected that when my prop fell aside and the door swung closed, he probably quit eating.

I was frustrated and discouraged, and worried about his health. Keeping weight on him was almost impossible; he was growing like a weed and his ribs stuck out like ripples in a pond. I had tried every trick known to entice his appetite, yet I could not put a layer of fat on him to protect him from the low outdoor temperatures.

To heighten my torment, each time I talked to Dave, he asked about Gilly. He saw the dog's potential and always offered to take Gil and give him the best that life could offer a bird dog. Gil would live in a house on a shooting preserve, be exercised daily in bird country, spend his days lounging in the editorial office, travel throughout the country on hunts, participate in trials and tests, and be by Dave's side everywhere he went. I imagined Gilly at the preserve, trembling on point with a noseful of hypnotic quail scent, wide-eyed and in a trance. Then I thought of him in his snow-topped doghouse, waiting for me to return from classes.

Late one Friday, with a heart like a shipwreck at sea, I called Dave and offered him the dog. I told him that whatever we did, we'd better do it quickly—before I got too weak to follow through.

The next day, I loaded Gilly and his favorite belongings into the wagon and headed for the office. When we arrived, Dave had everything ready for Gil: a new crate and bed cushion, new feeding bowls, and assorted bones and toys. Gil was happy to return to the office—one of his favorite places to visit—and ran about gaily, bent for joyful destruction and wreaking havoc wherever he could.

"Guess we should make this short and sweet," I said feebly, feeling a bit nauseated.

We stood for a moment and watched Gilly celebrate. Neither spoke for a while while he romped, terrorizing anything he thought he could get away with destroying. I broke the silence.

"We got a Thing, you know—he and I."

"I know."

Gilly grabbed a rawhide bone and carried it aloft, strutting down the hallway and growling at phantom littermates. Soon he returned without the bone, and I guessed that he had done what he'd done a hundred times before: He probably deposited it in a safe place while we talked—maybe changed his mind a time or two, sneaking from room to room to hide the bone where he thought no one would find it. He'd come out of the room into the hallway and look to see if anyone had noticed him carry it into the room. If he thought we had, he'd go back and get the bone and start all over.

"You'll keep in touch and tell me everything he does?"

Dave nodded silently at the request he'd heard the night before.

"I'd like to hunt with him sometime."

"We can do that."

"If anything ever happens and you can't keep him, he has to come back to me," I reiterated. "You can't sell him to anyone else without offering him to me first."

"You know I wouldn't."

"I know you wouldn't," I said, nodding apologetically.

We paused again as Gilly shredded pieces of cardboard, all that remained of an empty box he had selected to pulverize.

"I'd like a puppy out of him someday..."

"I told you you could have pick."

"I'm sorry. I guess I'm clinging, huh?" I said softly.

"Take your time," he said gently, and walked out of the room.

Alone with Gil, I squatted and looked at him. He immediately came over and leaned into me, putting all his weight against me, and slid down my legs, eventually turning upside down and flailing his legs about in comic relief. Since I didn't respond by rough-housing, he sat up and looked at me, and I rubbed both sides of his neck behind his ears.

Sensing the gravity of the moment, Gil offered a paw and leaned in to lick a salty rivulet from my cheek. Then, capricious as only a puppy can be, he pushed off me, grabbed a nearby tennis ball, and bounded away in an invitation to play.

Dave returned quietly to the room, and I stood to put on my coat. Gil stopped his rowdy sport, dropped his ball and looked me squarely in the eyes. Studying me, he cocked his head, and his tail sank slowly to the ground.

"Take care of him," I said lamely, my eyes riveted to the dog's.

"He'll have the best," Dave replied unnecessarily, his head turned away from mine.

There was nothing left to do but go. Gilly followed me to the door, but my silent wave told him I would be leaving alone. I let the door close slowly behind me and bent my head into the wind. I looked back only once, long enough to see Gilly's face in the window, his paws on the sill, with his new owner's hand resting on the back of his neck.

"Go make music, my Beethoven," I whispered.

John Holt *is a writer living in Whitefish, Montana with his wife, Lynda, three devoted kids—Jack, Elizabeth, and Rachel, a world-class tennis ball-fetching golden retriever named Zack, a new springer spaniel puppy named Bouchee, cats named Snowpoke and Hobbs, and an intellectual guinea pig known as Mickey.*

Holt writes regularly for publications that include Fly Fisherman, Men's Journal, Big Sky Journal, *and* The Denver Post. *He has a number of books in print including* Chasing Fish Tales: a Free-wheeling Year in the Life of an Angler *(Countrysport, 1993) and* Kicking Up Trouble—Upland Bird Hunting In The West *(Wilderness Adventures, 1994). Holt can be found fishing anywhere or bird hunting with good friends in the middle of nowhere.*

SOYBEAN, PHEASANTS, AND CRAWLING GORDONS

by John Holt

"The Damn Dog is on his knees again."

There was not much to see, just the black-and-tan wriggling rear end of the creature as he burrowed into a thick tangle of dried soybean stems, vines, leaves, and dead flowers. The Gordon was soon out of sight but we knew where he was. The slight undulations and quiverings of the cover, like a mouse cruising beneath soft, powdery snow in January, was a dead giveaway.

Early October anywhere is a fine time. This is especially so in southern Wisconsin. The muted golden, often crystalline light cast a surreal glow on the countryside. The gray of the soybean field seemed illuminated from within. So did the nearby fields of corn stubble. The overgrown drainage ditches that ran with the merest suggestion of an agrarian master plan also resonated to their own soft intensity. The land had gone electric in a gentle way.

Losing sight of the dog, Toby, was common for us by now. Trudging and pushing through the thick growth took effort and concentration. We were several days into a promising season. A routine was casually established. The dog was happy with his work and we were already sweating, only fifteen minutes along so far. We had not covered much ground and were some distance from late season conditioning. Our old farmhouse and ragged out-buildings were still visible on the oak-covered rise behind us.

The brush ahead was silent.

"Toby. Toby. Dammit where are you," my friend yelled. He loved dogs but hated whistles. They sound like Rush Street during rush hour he always groused. Still no dog. "Toby."

Then thirty feet ahead of us the brush began to bulge and grow towards the sky. Branches popped and cracked. I caught sight of a tail, an ear, perhaps a two-toned flank. Then madness, the kind that draws us out here to begin with, flashed full force in our faces. A cock pheasant blew straight up into the air in a riot of colors—emeralds, scarlets, browns, whites—wing beats, cackles. Toby was right behind the bird. Though moving quickly, the setter was a still life, sparkling eyes clearly focused on the game at hand.

This was not a flush, it was a full-tilt explosion.

The pheasant was maybe seven, eight feet high and starting to beat down and away from us. Then it crumpled to the ground.

"Christ, Holt, I didn't even get my gun up."

I do not remember anything about shooting the bird except for the vision of all that feathered color falling to earth. I'll never forget that or the sight of that wonderful Gordon setter sounding from the depths of the matted soybean world.

"Meyer. How are we ever going to find the bird."

"Hell, I can't even find the damn dog again."

We looked at each other and laughed. This *was* the Age of Aquarius. Why should bird hunting make anymore sense than anything else including that sophomoric musical? The media was still trying to explain Woodstock, Jefferson Airplane, communes, and Oaxacan pot. We were trying to stay sane amid the psychedelic confusion and the not so far off terror of Vietnam. My number in the draft lottery was seventy-seven. My friend's was just over one hundred. A couple of my friends had already been blown away over there. One came home maimed only to discover his wife long gone with a buddy of his. This could well be our last autumn together. We did not know what was waiting for us. The uncertainty and fear lent an intensity to the days in the field.

After a few seconds, Toby appeared from nowhere almost riding on top of the choking growth. In his mouth was the limp pheasant. Even with the life gone from them, ringnecks are spectacular sights. The setter brought the bird to my friend and

dropped it with a barely audible thump at his feet. Meyer picked it up, held it to the light, and then tossed the pheasant my way. Still warm and feeling heavy, a bit of blood curled from the bird's beak. I wiped it away, licking the residue from my forefinger. Slight taste of salt-copper. The sun was still shining, but the air was slightly cool on my face.

Toby glided over, totally at ease with the cover now. He looked at the pheasant and then at me and he was laughing, too. "We're living now, boss," he seemed to say. I was already addicted to fly fishing so spring and summer were shot for productive activities. I had always enjoyed birds, and now thanks to a fine dog it appeared that I was about to lose my autumns to upland shooting. In an uncommon flash of insight I realized, but not with alarm, that making a living was going to be a sporting proposition.

· · · · ·

Meyer and I rented the farmhouse somewhat west of a factory town called Beloit above the Wisconsin-Illinois line. The farmer still worked the 640 acres, rotating between corn, beans, and resting land. The farm was remote, perfect for a couple of clowns who liked loud music, whiskey, and a bit of nighttime gunfire. There was no one for miles and we were easily amused. This was not a gig grounded in responsibility. Meyer had already graduated from Ripon College and was working for the Milwaukee Road. I watched Toby, or he watched me, while my friend rode the rails. I was going to Beloit College studying creative writing and little else.

I don't think anyone would have considered us productive members of society. Not the types you invite to polite functions. That was fine with us. We were happy sitting around the farmhouse kitchen sipping whiskey from a couple of beer glasses that had found their way home from the Turtle Tap. A well-worn MEC reloader was bolted to a formica-topped table. Reloaded 12-gauge shells were stacked and scattered about in prodigious numbers. If the revolution was coming, and the Beatles said it was, we were ready.

Actually our objectives were more conventional. In addition to hunting the fields four or five times a week, we also staged regular live pigeon shoots. The decrepit barn still held count-less bales of old straw. Nearby rusty bins were filled to overflow-ing with tons of field-dried corn. Word about this accessible grain spread to better pigeon circles in the Beloit area. There were hundreds of the gray birds perched in the barn. Our farmer hated the damage they wreaked on his corn, which he fed to beef cattle on another operation he owned down the road. We were encouraged to cull the pigeon flock to the extent that powder, shot, plastic wads, primers, and occasionally wrapped chunks of prime beef appeared regularly on our crumbling cement doorstep.

The farm was a wondrous thing to behold when pulling into the yard late at night in Meyer's old but highly polished black Eldorado after another evening unsuccessfully trying to pick up girls in Beloit. Meyer was over seven feet tall. I was over six. The farm had a reputation for gunfire. We usually drove home alone.

The three of us would head out to the barn, normally in the early afternoon. A dysfunctional silo—metaphor everywhere we looked it seemed—opened into the barn. We had sealed all openings between the barn and the silo and hammered boards over the most obvious openings in the barn. In other words, the only easy way out of the structure during moments of avian panic was through a wide opening in the silo's metal cap.

One of us would work his way to the upper level of the barn and begin raising hell. The flappings of seriously upset birds would soon build to a tumultuous uproar. Then the pigeons would go crazy and take flight. A steady stream of them would burst from the silo—our own personal high tower. We'd shoot forever, trading places every so often. Toby truly enjoyed him-self retrieving the fallen birds and dropping them into what quickly became an impressive pile. The setter went crazy when-ever we grabbed our guns, whenever we started shooting. His square snout would work the air, sucking in deep draughts of air perfumed with gunsmoke. He was one of us. Meyer and I knew that there was top-notch bird dog lurking just below the surface in Toby. Time would prove the acuity of our assessment.

We breasted a number of the pigeons, sauteing them in butter, garlic, and white wine. But even Toby grew tired of the meat after a while. We turned to other methods of disposal. They loved our weekly pigeon drops at the county dump.

"You boys ever do anythin' sides blast dem pigeons?"

"Do you think we should?"

"Naw. You two look to be stretched pretty tight already."

And life rolled on toward somewhere.

We never tired of this sport and actually became fair shooters. The farmer was grateful. But if there is a hell, I'm sure there will be pigeons waiting for me. I hope Meyer can make the trip.

That is what I meant about not remembering the shot that dropped the pheasant. The hunting by this time was instinctive. The 870 came up only slightly behind the flush, quickly making up the disparity; most of the time the bird crumpled. The stalking and anticipation, especially with Toby digging through the soybeans or traversing the corn stubble, was always keen. The shooting became predatory and that developed into its own type of satisfaction. The same pleasure exists when I fish for weeks on end. The mind instantly measures the water and the cast needed, and the body executes the commands with dispatch. The sight of a wild brown trout hammering an Elk Hair caddis is the rush, like watching the pheasant tumble from the sky.

· · · · ·

Meyer took a lot of grief from his father, a confirmed golden Lab man, after he drove out to a farm near Madison and picked up the Gordon puppy one spring day.

"The breed is too slow."

"You can't teach them anything. All they ever do is follow their nose."

"Nobody hunts with them anymore."

"You'll never see the dog with all that black coat."

And on and on.

Meyer was not fazed. This was the kind of dog he wanted and now he had one. The first autumn, before we had the farm, most of our hunting was spent with Meyer yelling "Toby, goddammit. Come back here. Dammit." And we'd watch the setter romp to his heart's content, pheasants flying everywhere, well out of range. We spent hours working with the eager dog who never seemed to tire of a game that he instinctively understood on a level far more basic than we did. His enthusiasm and willingness to please taught me a good deal about bird hunting. Toby would never "knock 'em dead" at a trial, but then neither Meyer nor I would ever make an Olympic shooting team. None of this mattered to the dog or to us, really. Toby led the way down the meandering path of that freeform autumn, a time where we became friends as one, sharing moments in the field beyond words. The sight of that Gordon charging about the thick cover, tail wagging, coat shining in subdued light was glorious. Even without all of the pheasants, we would have been satisfied.

Then one day Meyer came in from the field, flushed, wired. Something had changed. You could see it in his eyes.

"Holt, I told ya Toby'd catch on. Just needed time. He works right in front now. Perfect pace. Back and forth. Thorough. Tomorrow you'll see."

And I did. We hunted the land surrounding the farm. Toby stayed in tight picking up the scent that drifted on complicated seams of air. Or he exhibited that first embryonic down-on-his-knees, whatever-it-takes-to-move-the-bird intensity. He moved steadily with an air of confidence and he kicked up birds. We each shot our limit and the dog retrieved them without a hitch.

"Meyer. This ain't the same dog."

"Tell me something new. All the yelling. Maybe he even learned from watching me pick up so many pheasants. I haven't a clue. It's just there. Holto, I got a bird dog."

Meyer always called me Holto when he was pleased with himself and he was grinning brightly right now. It was a fine sight that still makes me laugh a little whenever I recall the moment. This is not to say that Toby had miraculously turned perfect. None of us ever do, and there were days when that dog would romp so far off in the field that we thought about filing a missing persons report. But for all of this, he had pretty much turned abruptly into an excellent bird dog. There were even times when he would come to point, a difficult task on the springy carpet of dead bean vines. The pheasants knew they were safe holding down deep in the cover. Eventually Toby would forsake the purity of his breed and dive into the brush in a pell-mell maelstrom of paws, legs, and vibrating tail. Soon enough the colorful birds would explode once again from the sere tangle with Toby close behind. Anticipating where the pheasants and that wild dog would surface was exciting sport.

We were in heaven, the three of us, and even Meyer's dad admitted, barely, that Toby had turned out to be a good dog in the field. We had things made. Meyer made good money from the railroad; I brought in enough from a bartending job. Toby had the land to roam and all those birds to chase. Life was sweet that fall.

We hunted almost every day of the season. The land was rich, filled with birds. There were so many hens that a couple of hundred cocks would be needed to handle the procreational responsibilities. Or so it seemed. A biologist told Meyer that the fields of soybeans were a magnet for pheasants throughout the valley. Trying to estimate populations was futile. Unrealistic. Unnecessary. The fact that we had all of these birds was sufficient. For every male flushed, a dozen females broke cover, bursting quickly in small brown-gray groups that cackled and squawked in demure imitation of their flashier companions. At first Toby could not understand why we did not shoot the hens. After all, to a dog's nose a pheasant is a pheasant. But he soon learned, though I am convinced that on those rare afternoons when cocks were rare finds, Toby would have liked one of us to drop a hen. I know how he felt.

Regardless, that autumn at the farm was, by a long shot, the best season of bird hunting I've ever experienced. Meyer moved to Washington and I moved to Montana. Toby is, of course, long gone.

. . . . .

A couple of decades and some bar change have passed by since those intense times. Still, while walking the nearly unimaginable openness of central Montana hunting sharptails or working a ridge chasing blues, those days on that Wisconsin farm come to mind. Particularly the one where Toby first crawled after a bird and showed me what his kind of dog was about.

After that first bursting shot, the outing was filled with hens that I swung through but never shot and several more brightly colored cocks that Meyer and I did shoot. The sun moved into a western bank of clouds. We decided to head back up hill to the warm kitchen.

"Holto, we've still got a virgin bottle of Jim Beam rye. You mix a few cocktails and we'll sip them like civilized folks while I fry up the birds in a little butter, some sage, a little brandy..."

"Right Meyer. You want yours in a mug or a tumbler."

"Don't forget the ice."

"One cube or two?"

We were nearing the yard and Toby had vanished. We pushed on in silence.

Twenty yards from the barn the cover tore apart and a cock broke free with Toby in pursuit. We both raised our guns. Neither of us fired a shot. Toby stopped. The three of us watched the pheasant flash downwind in the last golden light of sunset.

Stuart Williams has had a birdshooting career as extensive as it has been intensive, with over one hundred trips to twenty-four countries. He got his start with hunting dogs at a very early age, shooting quail over a brace of his uncle's grand setters. Later he trained Brittany spaniels. He has shot quail over pointers on classic Georgia plantations and in the brush of south Texas; partridges over pointers in the Andes of Peru and Ecuador; pheasants over Drahthaars in Bulgaria; and pheasants, chukars, and Hungarian partridges over springer spaniels in Turkey. His favorite birdshooting destination is Argentina, which he has visited twenty-four times.

Williams is a regular contributor to Gun Dog, Wing and Shot, Shooting Sportsman, Sporting Clays, *and other publications. He is international editor of* Hunting Report, Birdshooters' Edition. *His major work is* Birds on the Horizon: Wingshooting Adventures Around the World, *published by Countrysport Press.*

INTERNATIONAL BIRD DOGS

by Stuart Williams

Considered on a worldwide basis, shooting birds over dogs has fallen on evil days. Aside from the United States and Canada, "dogging" is commonly practiced in just four countries: Mexico, Argentina, Uruguay, and Scotland.

The chaparral, or brush, of Tamaulipas state in northeastern Mexico offers the finest quail shooting that I hope to see in this world or the next. Almost every plant there grows in enmity to the flesh of man: *cholla, nopal, yucca,*

Spanish dagger and, most malevolent of all, *tasajilla,* a pencil-shaped cactus that, the more you try to free yourself from it, the more deeply it impales you. There is no more protective quail cover anywhere.

Where the brush has been cleared away the land has been planted in corn and sorghum and sunflowers. Under the *ejido,* or cooperative, system of farming, which is based on a socialist model and is thus highly inefficient, lots of grain and seeds are never harvested and much is wasted on the ground. It is a kind of benign neglect, and the quail love it. A team of wildlife biologists with unlimited funds could not create better conditions for bobwhite quail.

Over the years I have hunted quail in Tamaulipas a dozen times, but of those dozen times the season of 1992-93 certainly shines as the finest. In the spring and summer of 1992 Tamaulipas received the heaviest rainfalls in many years, and quail populations exploded in response. When I shot whitewing doves there in September 1992, I routinely saw twenty to twenty-five coveys every day just traveling to and from the dove fields.

In December of that year I shot quail out of El Tejón, a lodge long known for the consistently high quality of shooting it produces. The first afternoon David Gregory—booking agent and hunting impresario par excellence—and I enjoyed a slam dunk of a quail shoot with David McBee, a well-known dog handler from Texas.

The previous day he had scouted a field where he had seen twelve coveys in the last fifteen minutes of daylight. That is the field we would hunt.

On the first day conditions were perfect: temperature in the 60s, a breeze of eight to ten miles per hour, and vegetation that had been moistened to the proper degree by an early morning drizzle.

Upon arrival in The Happy Hunting Grounds, McBee put down Jodie and Queenie, pointers; Ruby, a German shorthair; and Annie, a setter. We worked a fallow field about one-half mile square, grown up in mixed weeds, wild daisies, and wild *tomatillos,* or miniature green tomatoes, the seeds of which quail love.

Annie made game within fifty yards of the truck, and Jodie backed. The birds were evidently running because time and again Annie would move forward and readjust her point. Then Jodie got in the game, moving ahead of Annie as the birds ran ahead. Some of the way the dogs moved forward side by side precisely in step. I have seen some extraordinary dog work but never anything like that. The dogs kept up this relay for nearly

100 yards until the birds could stand the pressure no longer. They flushed just ahead of Jodie's nose; I took two birds from air and David Gregory one.

On the next point Ruby, the shorthair, made game solidly. I moved in quickly but before I could get close she laid down on her belly, continuing to point rigidly. I stepped in front of her, a single rocketed away, and I put it down.

On the next point two birds got up and flew to the left and right, respectively. I put down the left bird and Gregory the right bird at precisely the same instant as McBee shouted his applause.

For the most part the birds were difficult to see and shoot that afternoon because they simply wouldn't fly high enough to make themselves visible against the sky. We did, however, make a number of long shots on low, crossing birds that dropped in long slants, and finished the day with fifty birds.

The next afternoon Eduardo "Lalo" Maraboto, manager of El Sargento Lodge, joined me. McBee manipulated the mutts and Gregory immortalized the grand deeds with his cameras.

We went out to a ranch of rolling hills covered with a dense yellow carpet of wild daisies, and with recently harvested sorghum and tall grass. For the first two hours we concentrated primarily on photography.

The final hour was perhaps the finest hour of quail shooting I have ever enjoyed. McBee put down Jodie, Annie, and Diamond, a littermate of Jodie's, in a weed field of about sixty acres surrounded by dense thornbrush and cactus. In the final hour the dogs moved just five very large coveys, but between the covey rises they pointed singles almost continuously. I counted thirty-five points, and undoubtedly missed some. Many times all three dogs were on point. Annie would have a bird, Jodie another 100 yards away, and Diamond still another 135 yards away in a different direction. At other times all three dogs would be pointing the same bird, surrounding it in triangular fashion. Many of the birds were runners, and the dogs—sometimes two, sometimes all three—would continuously move forward with them, side by side precisely in step. In the cool fragrant gloom of evening birds roared up and away, and shooting and shouting filled the air with a joyous cacophony. It ended all too soon, as all good things do, when we could no longer see to shoot. The dogs were still pointing in the thickening darkness and they hated to give it up. With difficulty did McBee get them back into the truck.

During the course of that evening I saw some of the most elegant, disciplined, exhilarating dog work I hope to see in this world or the next; tails rigidly erect, mouths tightly shut, bodies quivering with excitement like a high tension wire, leaning toward the bird with head well extended, honoring and backing with perfect teamwork, all beyond reproach.

In January 1993 I returned to Tamaulipas, this time to shoot at No Le Hace Lodge, an opulent shooting resort built by Lloyd Bentsen, Sr., in the middle 1960s. It was originally intended to be a corporate entertainment retreat for the oil industry. Now it is open to the public.

During the 1992-93 season No Le Hace Lodge retained Gerry Glasco as head dog handler. Gerry annually trucks about forty dogs and two assistant dog handlers to Mexico for the quail season. He is the only handler in Mexico who has enough dogs to keep four fully finished, fresh dogs on the ground at all times for each party of two shooters. (He calls them his four dog dragnet.) I have shot with him at times when he had no less than seven dogs on the ground—all pointing at the same time.

The first three days at No Le Hace I shot with Mike Fitzgerald II, director of Mexican programs for Fish and Game Frontiers of Wexford, Pennsylvania. Then Mike left, and on the fourth day I went out with Glasco and his assistant dog handler, Joe Dan Carter, who were taking a busman's holiday. We drove far to the west, arriving at the field of choice just at sunrise. Conditions were perfect: a heavy dew, temperature in the 60s, a gentle breeze, excellent cover, and plenty of food. Gerry put down his dragnet, and they sifted through every centimeter of cover. Suddenly one dog pointed and the others were immediately paralyzed in response. I moved ahead, a small covey leaped into air, and I shot two birds going straight away.

As soon as the sun climbed a ways in the sky, the heat forced the birds to take refuge in the cool shade of the dense fencerows, or *cortinas.*

At the first *cortina* Gerry put down Buck, a setter, and Radar, a Drahthaar, his two most finished dogs. I went down the left side and Joe Dan down the right, and Gerry followed in his truck. A covey exploded out to my side, and I took down two birds with the first shot and one with the second for a two-shot triple. A bit further Buck pointed, and I dropped a bird that got up high and tried to fly back over my head. Every minute or so the dogs would make game, and in ten minutes we shot more birds than in the previous two hours. On one flurry Joe Dan and I put down six birds in as many seconds, and Radar retrieved two at a time—something I had never seen before.

Much of the time I rode on the specially built bucket seats which were mounted on the front of the truck. They greatly facilitated getting into action. When we called it a morning at 1:30 p.m. we had seventy-six birds picked up.

We headed to San Fernando, the closest town of any size, for lunch. We ate at an excellent small restaurant called Los Caporales, where Gerry regularly took his clients. We started out with their famous appetizer, *queso flameado*, which is a dense melted cheese flavored with sausage drippings. Smeared on tortillas, it is absolutely irresistible. We moved on to the house specialty, the *Parilla los Caporales*, a mixed grill of sweetbreads, short ribs, pieces of chicken, and chunks of sausage. The finale of the feast was cheesecake, and lemon meringue pie with graham cracker crust—the best I ever tasted. We washed it all down with Bohemia, that wonderful Mexican beer. Gerry said that the feast had been "mighty high-powered hoggings," and he should certainly know, because he is a pig farmer in the off season.

However, it was not lunch, but the last hour of the day that was *la mejor hora del dia*—the best hour of the day. Gerry put down his dragnet of dogs in a mile-long field of harvested sorghum overgrown with crabgrass and weeds, parallel to a dense thicket of cactus and thornbrush. I rode in the right bucket seat and Gerry in the left while Joe Dan drove along the edge of the thicket. On the first covey rise the birds flew right in front of us towards the thicket. I took down two with my first shot and one with my second. Gerry emptied his eight-shot

Benelli, and empty shells kept hitting me in the face, but nary a bird did I see fall.

Then Gerry and Joe Dan got down and walked, Gerry about fifty yards out and Joe Dan about one hundred yards out from the brush, all of us following a parallel course, while I continued to ride up on the front of the truck. A Mexican boy drove. As the dogs pointed and the birds flushed, they would invariably fly toward the brush, thus passing over or to the side of me. I was the beneficiary of what you might call a driven quail shoot. On one covey rise a dozen birds flew over high, and I knocked down one stone dead from forty yards up. It fell in the midst of the thornbrush, and *mirabile dictu*, a birdboy crawled on his belly far into that brush and fetched it.

Then came the high point of the day for me. Two dogs pointed, Gerry put up the birds, and they came right toward the truck. While the truck was still moving I took down a bird to my left, which fell far behind the truck, and then one to the right, which fell far in front. Gerry missed a low bird, which crossed in front of me at forty yards, and I snatched it down in the waning light. In one day I had become a master drive-by quail shooter.

I shall never forget the last delightful hour of that day: riding up on the front of the truck, with waves of cool, delicious air washing over me; the dogs quartering back and forth, searching out bird scent; birds bursting into air on all sides; and shotguns roaring out their peremptory orders to cease and desist from flight—all of it laid out before me like a grand show enacted for an emperor riding in his chariot.

The dogs wanted to hunt into the darkness, and we had to collect them using the headlights. In fact, we shot the last covey rise in the light of the high beams. We finished the day with 143 birds picked up—my best day of quail shooting ever.

That may seem like a lot of birds, and it is, but the average life expectancy of a quail in the Tamaulipas brush is only about $1^1/_2$ years, so even very intensive shooting by the very few shooters who go down that way doesn't even replace the natural rate of mortality.

The rolling grasslands of Argentina and Uruguay are home of the tailless tinamou partridge, one of the world's great game birds. The tinamou is a drab brown bird about twice the size of the bobwhite quail that thrives in fields of short grass and sparse cover and is therefore dependent on man and cattle for its well-being. To the upland hunter whose experience is with pheasants, ruffed grouse, and bobwhite quail, it would scarcely seem credible that a game bird would inhabit fields with grass so short and cover so thin that they would hardly hide a sparrow. Yet the tinamou is a different kind of bird altogether. It is primarily a running bird, not a flying one, and thick cover would impede its movement as well as block its view of avian enemies. Finally, it is so perfectly camouflaged that it hardly needs any cover at all. I have on many occasions seen a dog go on point out on bare ground where I could have sworn there wasn't a bird within half a mile. Yet in every instance there was indeed a bird there.

The tinamou is an even more incorrigible runner than the pheasant. It simply will not fly unless hunter and dog put firm and consistent pressure on it—usually after it has run at least fifty yards, sometimes over one hundred yards, from the place where it was pointed. Furthermore, when it does get up, it blasts off with such explosiveness that it leaves the inexperienced gunner haplessly blowing holes in the air.

The tinamou feeds and moves about singly. I have never seen a simultaneous double, or even a consecutive double. I have, however, on several occasions got into a hot corner where I had six to eight flushes in rapid succession. There is simply nothing in the world of upland shooting to compare with this experience.

Shoot operators use pointers almost exclusively. These dogs are anything but field-trial dogs. They work in close, and when they make game and the tinamou runs out ahead of them, they creep forward, quickly readjusting their point as they go. A staunch dog is totally worthless on tinamou.

Because tinamou usually get up at considerable distance and get away quite rapidly, shooting them is strictly a 12-gauge game. The little 20- and 28-bore guns affected by "gentlemen" gunners in this country will quickly put you out of the tinamou game. I like an over-under with barrels at least twenty-eight inches long bored modified and full, or a semi-auto with twenty-eight inch barrel with modified choke tube.

The best load is one throwing a full $1^1/_4$ ounces of nickel-plated 7s or buffered, cooper-plated 7s. Fired out of a modified or full choke gun, any of these loads will cleanly kill tinamou at forty yards.

I have shot tinamou at the world-renowned Estancia Santa Emilia in Uruguay, out of the opulent Goya Lodge in the rice-growing country of Corrientes Province in northeastern Argentina, and in the fertile fields of the Río Negro Valley in south-central Argentina. I had one of my most memorable shoots with outfitter Carlos Sanchez in the lush uplands of Entre Riós Province, which lies between the might Uruguay and Paraná rivers.

We were working through a field of emerald-green grass not six inches high. Quartering back and forth into the breeze were Carlos's pointers, Ossie and Camila, most efficient meat dogs. Suddenly Ossie stopped in midstride, and his body quivered as if ten thousand volts of electricity were flowing through it. Camila backed and honored.

Carlos ordered: "Move out smartly in front of Ossie and take the bird!"

The bird, however, did not cooperate. I stepped out smartly, but Ossie broke point and crept forward five yards and pointed again. I moved up ahead of him, and he again moved forward and pointed. Clearly we were dealing with a runner.

Carlos exhorted: "Move out faster or the bird will just run away from you!"

I walked as fast as I could for twenty-five yards, and a brown bombshell exploded underfoot and rocketed off low and straight. I dropped the bird softly on to the grass at thirty-five yards. Ossie and Camila raced to fetch.

Within minutes Camila had another bird, and Ossie backed precisely, tail extended straight back in the European manner. Clearly this bird was also a runner, because Camila broke point and raced forward and pointed again. Then Ossie dashed in front of her and pointed for a few seconds, and Camila once again raced out ahead and pointed. Some of the way they crept forward side by side. They kept up this pas de deux for nearly one hundred yards, while Carlos continually urged me: "Get out ahead of the dogs! Put pressure on the bird! Bear down on the bird! Make it fly!"

I did precisely that, and after 125 yards of this footrace the bird could stand the pressure no longer. It burst into air, headed out over a fence toward a road, and I dropped it squarely in the middle of the road. Ossie snaked under the fence, grabbed the bird, and sailed back over the fence.

On the next point I almost had to run ahead of the dogs to make the bird fly, and when it did get up it was a full forty yards in front. It likewise veered off towards the road, and I sent three shots after it. Not a hint did it show of a hit, but nonetheless I felt sure that all three shots had been well delivered. Surely enough, just as the bird reached the adjacent field it began to falter. It flew another one hundred yards and dropped stone dead. Carlos and his dog handler and I gave out a shout. The dog handler marked it down precisely, crossed two fences, walked two hundred yards, bent down, and picked it up without searching in the least.

Then two birds got up wild in rapid succession at thirty to forty-five yards, and I laid them both on the grass. The shooting kept up like this for about three hours. The final action capped off the morning in a most spectacular and satisfying manner. The dogs made game, the bird raced out ahead, and the dogs ran along with it until they forced it to fly at thirty yards, squarely between them. The bird flew straight up, and at the apex of its flight I plucked it back down to earth. Ossie snatched it out of midair.

It had been a near-perfect morning. The heavy dew held bird scent wondrously well, hanging in pearls from every blade of grass. Along the edges of the field enormous windbreak Lombardy popular and eucalyptus and drunken, or *palo borracho*, trees swayed in the cloudless sky, and the limbs of the *ombu* trees reached out chaotically in all directions. The mid-winter temperature was a perfect sixty-seven degrees, and the air was filled with a most exhilarating fragrance, even though I could not discern a single flower. It was a rare and wonderful day to be alive and afield.

We moved back to the grand manor house at Estancia El Garbón for lunch. Helen Calderón, lady of the manor, served a magnificent luncheon. She started out with a fine quiche of eggs, bacon, and nettle leaves; followed that with roast pork, pureed spinach, and roast potatoes; and topped off the feast with peach upside-down cake à la mode. Carlos and I grunted most contentedly as we staggered back to our rooms for a siesta.

Such are the delights of shooting tinamou in the fertile farmlands of Uruguay and Argentina.

. . . . .

Shooting Scottish grouse on the heather-covered moors of Scotland over dogs, or "dogging," as it is commonly known, has long been the poor cousin of shooting driven grouse. It simply does not have the mystique, prestige, or cachet of driven grouse shooting, and it permits the shooter to kill only a fraction of the birds he might get on a day of driving. Nevertheless, dogging has its devotees, who stoutly maintain that it is a superior sport to driving.

Dogging is generally practiced only in the northern parts of Scotland, in Sutherland and Caithness. There the number of birds are insufficient to justify the high costs of driving. It is also practiced on other moors where the lay of the land does not permit driving. It is used as a technique to herd the birds away from the periphery of the moor to the inner areas where they are more easily controlled. Finally, it is practiced in the first week of the season to agitate the birds—especially the young birds—and make them wilder so that they will fly better when the driving begins.

English setters and pointers are far and away the most commonly used breeds. Other breeds occasionally seen are Gordon and Irish setters, springer spaniels, and the so-called versatile dogs: German shorthairs, vizslas, and Weimaraners. These dogs find the birds. After the birds have been shot, other breeds, yellow and black Labs, move in and retrieve. There is generally a strict division of labor, especially if pointers and setters are used. If in the exceptional case that one or more of the versatile breeds are used, they might also do the retrieving.

Dogging fell into neglect for many years but is now enjoying something of a comeback. To a great extent that is because shooting driven grouse has become hideously expensive. One can enjoy a day of sport over the dogs for a fraction of what a day of driven shooting costs.

I had the good fortune to enjoy a week of dogging at the famous Seafield Sportings Club—alas a destination of the past—in Banffshire, Scotland, several years back. I shot with two fellow Americans, Jim Walter and Burke Kibler, and George Drummond, a dog handler known far and wide for his beautifully trained springer spaniels. The estate manager, Colin Whittle, completed the foursome.

On the first day—a beautiful day—George put down a brace of his irrepressible dogs, Jack and Lady, and a lady dog handler put down a brace of Irish setters (which are almost never seen afield in Scotland nowadays). Colin and I shot with George Drummond, and Burke and Jim with the lady dog handler. Keepers followed Jim and Burke with black Labs to pick up fallen birds.

The date was the Twelfth of August, the opening of the grouse season and the most sacrosanct date on the British sporting calendar. The heather was at the peak of its violet bloom. As we waded through it, it enveloped us with a mellow fragrance.

Colin and I had not gone two hundred yards when the urgent wagging of the spaniels' tails commanded our close attention. George blew a shrill blast on his whistle:

"Mark, mark, sirs, there'll be birds just ahead of ye here! A covey, I should think!"

Just then the covey lifted up out of the heather, and Colin and I put down birds simultaneously. I dispatched a second futile shot just as the birds were getting out of range. The covey sailed away down the slope, skimming along just over the heather.

"Not a bad beginning at all!" George commented. Jack and Lady each dumped a bird at his feet and climbed up on him seeking approbation. After a couple of pats he sent them back to work.

"Doun, laddie, doun, doun! Doun, garrl, doun!"

Within 150 yards those tails went into paroxysms again. This time the birds, evidently young and uninitiated, held closely.

Then they arose and scooted out across the heather. I killed one bird and wounded a second with my first shot and put it down cleanly with the second shot.

"What a lovely right and left, sir!"

On the next flush a huge pack of birds got up in staggered fashion. Colin and I each doubled, reloaded, and took down a third bird. The birds unwisely swung downhill, arrogantly uttering their "go-back! go-back! go-back!" as they went. George blew a warning blast, and the birds flew right over Jim and Burke. They were ready, and pulled down three birds with four shots. Nine birds in as many seconds! There were wild congratulations all around.

"Lovely gunwork, sirs, lovely gunwork!"

"Oh aye, oh aye! That it was indeed! Very rare gunwork!"

The whole force of Labs and springers nosed out the heather for fallen birds.

By lunchtime we had 17$\frac{1}{2}$ brace of birds—a very respectable start for the Glorious Twelfth.

We sprawled out languorously in the heather and feasted on smoked salmon on pumpernickel sandwiches; caviar on black bread; cold sliced Prague ham; Stilton and Port Salut cheeses; champagne grapes; a crisp salad; and a good Pouilly Fuissé and Beaujolais to wash it all down. Afterwards, sated and dulled by the rich foods, relaxed by the wines, and warmed by the sun, we dozed on the fragrant hillside.

A half hour later I was awakened by an enormous Lab giving me a sloppy kiss on the ear. I sat up reflecting on that line of Shakespeare: "Thou hast neither youth nor age, but as it were an after-dinner sleep, dreaming on both."

Thomas BeVier *was raised on an Ohio farm in the 1950s, and it was there that he shot his first pheasant and woodcock in front of his first dog, a Brittany spaniel, with an old J.C. Higgins 12-gauge shotgun, which he still owns.*

When barely out of his teens, he went to work for his first newspaper, The Lorain *(Ohio)* Journal. *Later he worked for newspapers in Oklahoma, where he learned about shooting quail from horseback, in Tennessee, where he had a brief flirtation with pointers, and in Michigan, where he has renewed his association with Brittanies.*

For the last decade he has covered the northern Lower Peninsula and the Upper Peninsula of Michigan for the Detroit Free Press *and the* Detroit News. *He has also written for various magazines.*

THIS IS WHAT IT'S ALL ABOUT ALFIE

by Thomas BeVier

I am a modest man. Just ask anyone who knows me.

They will tell you, for instance, that only occasionally do they catch me boasting that my wife is the best cook north of Toledo. Nor do they hear me extolling the virtues of my two sons, although the boys have met all reasonable expectations for this day and time, having each served only one overnight jail term. My hubris is so contained that I usually resist informing fellow anglers that catching a muskie is not a big deal by reminding them that I got mine the first time out.

And so, with the understanding that braggadocio is a minor function of my character, I may be excused for stating that when it comes to dogs, I have few peers. I am confident my current Dog in Residence, a bonnie Brittany called Francie, would bear out the claim.

(A digression and an explanation for those who may wonder how I came up with a name like Francie for my dog: Francie is my wife's middle name. When things are rocky on the domestic front, I find it constructive to vent anger by simply calling my dog. "Come Francie, you bitch," I holler from the back stoop. Francie the dog doesn't mind, and Francie the spouse is always well out of earshot.)

My rationalization for an uncommon breach of modesty is that it is needed as a preamble to telling about Alfie, a pointer of refined bloodlines and noble bearing about whom it is difficult to compliment further. There will be more said about him in due time.

And there is this: Perhaps, by recognizing my considerable skills with dogs, others who have squandered their precious time and considerable sums of money because they believed, completely and unquestioningly as I did, in the general goodness of dogs, from the lowest mongrel even unto the Best of Westminster or Grand Junction, will find comfort from my experience with Alfie.

So my motive is pure when I say that dogs come when I call them, that they sit before me as willing vassals, wagging and never jumping up, and that rare is the one that doesn't quickly surrender to disciplined heeling with me on the other end of the lead. Also, that I easily calm puppy fervor, the stupidity of studs, or the raised hackles of a one of those barking monsters unleashed on visitors by a boorish owner. A raised hand, palm out, unthreateningly, or a sharp word is all it takes. Firm but friendly, that's my style. With dogs, I am the boss I have never personally had: kind and rewarding most of the time, charitable and constructive with criticism, patient and understanding in the face of failure.

Francie, I should note, is the ultimate benficiary of my gift, standing as she does at the head of a long line of canine friends who have enriched my life from puberty onward toward initiation into the American Association of Retired Persons. But much as I adore her, this story is not about Francie. That is because she is perfection, with a certain allowance for being firecracker-shy and thunderstorm-shy, as well as a bit gun-shy.

The first rule of journalism, my chosen trade, says that stories about perfection aren't worth printing. Alas, it's a waste of ink to write about the honest politician, the straight-arrow car dealer, or the understanding cop. "Give us good news," readers choir, but they don't mean it. What they really want is stories about blood and gore, malfeasance at all levels of gov-

ernment and finance, and the petty failures of their sports and entertainment heroes. Failing any of that, they'll settle for saccharine reports on the misfortunes of their neighbors.

I assume the general reader's crass appetite extends to stories about dogs. And for that, fortunately, I presume, I remember Alfie.

· · · · ·

"What's it all about, Alfie?" It was one of the pressing questions of the era, an era fulsome with questions both great and small. Dionne Warwich sang the song, and a previous wife had a crush on Michael Caine, who starred in the movie.

Alfie came to me as a puppy, like all the other dogs I've owned. As a matter of fact, I can reckon my life in puppies. There are other ways to take an accounting, of course. Children or jobs could serve as a basis. I read someplace that one's life can even be counted out in coffee spoons. I prefer puppies.

There are disappointments with children or jobs, and coffee is bitter. A puppy has never let me down, not even Alfie. That he failed me (Or—this essay's cosmic question—did I fail him?) in his adolescence and early manhood is beside the point. As a puppy he was great. All puppies are great.

When I bought Alfie, I was living in the deep South, land of barbecue, antebellum architecture and politics, and—best of all—coveys of very shootable quail. Growing up in Ohio, I had hunted pheasant, woodcock, and ducks, but only when I flushed my first quail did I experience a wingshooter's epiphany.

I was introduced to quail by the sheriff of a rural county, a gentle and thoughtful man, the likes of whom has so often been put to slander in films and commercials. It's true that his shotgun of choice in the field was the riot gun from his patrol car, a weapon several inches short of legal which threw a fearsomely broad pattern, but in all other regards he was a true sportsman.

"I'll tell you why I hunt," he drawled. "It's to watch the dogs work. I just love watching my dogs work."

What dogs they were—four pointers, two males and two bitches, as I recall, and all distantly related. I had never seen such dogs, honed to muscle and bone, conditioned beyond conditioning. They were houndlike in repose, lanquid as a Delta evening or their master's voice. But loose them from the cages on the pickup truck, and they were immediately transformed. They danced, almost feline in their grace, and then with a word from the sheriff they were off, running on the edge of control.

On the edge of control...but never out of control. With a whistle, but mostly with hand commands, the sheriff guided them in the hunt, moving them left and right to quarter the wind, motioning them back when they ranged too far. Ballets have been performed less artfully. And then they'd strike a scent, and sometimes a dog would be so eager to come to point that he'd tumble head over heels before freezing into the classic, shivering pose.

"Easy, easy," the sheriff would drone as we moved through the cover, and the dogs would hold. Then, in that whir of wing and motion that always surpasses expectation, the birds would flush. The guns would sound. Birds would drop. The dogs would fetch them.

"So sheriff," I said, "Where can I get a dog like yours?"

"Son, dogs like these are made not born. It takes a lot of work and patience to make a good dog. No offense intended, but I don't know if you're up to it."

I informed him that I had trained a half dozen dogs, and that while only one of them had been a bird dog I was sure I wouldn't have any trouble with a pointer. Against his better judgment, I suppose, he gave me the name of his breeder. "Tell him I sent you, and, oh yeh, take money," he said.

I expected to pay maybe as much as $200. Forget it. Talk about sticker shock. "You get what you pay for," the breeder told me. To this day, I confess only to my closest friends how much I paid for Alfie. I never did tell my wife. Actually, I lied when she asked. We were later divorced. What can I say?

He was a fine looking dog, deep-chested, long in the leg and with head found only in the pure of breed. And energy. Even as a puppy, Alfie could tire five children at play. He'd go on point on a quail wing dangled from a string from the very beginning.

Friends dropped by. "Fine dog," they'd say. "How much did you pay for him? When are you going to start training him?"

I built him a house and pen. Alfie was not a pet, I told my brood. "He's a hunting dog," I advised them. He chewed his way out of the pen to chase them around the yard. Then he climbed the chain link fence and ran away. It took hours to find him.

Serious training started early, perhaps too early as I think back. He was a quick learner. Come. Sit. Heel. He learned easily, easier than any other dog I'd ever had. But the minute I'd take him off a lead he'd run away, hell bent for who knows where.

Leads became progressively longer until we were so strung out I felt foolish. Fifty feet of nylon cord is an unwieldy lot. I'd work him mornings and afternoons. He'd respond to voice commands, hand signals, and a whistle. He found birds. But each time I'd take him off the lead, he'd run off.

"My dog ran away," I'd explain to my boss when I was late to work. It happened so frequently that it became a joke around the office.

"Where's BeVier?" the city editor would ask.

"Chasing his dog," somebody would respond.

A year passed. Alfie was still running away. I was at my wit's end. I'd paid so much for him and invested so much time. I was beyond pride and into disappointment.

And so I gave him to my friend Charlie, with the proviso that he'd take me hunting when he got Alfie properly trained.

Charlie was confident. "I never saw a dog I couldn't train," he said. "The problem with you is that you coddle him. You've got to be firm."

I shrugged. I'd tried both coddling and firmness with the same results. Alfie always ran away.

A week passed. I called my friend.

"How's Alfie doing?" I asked.

"Fine. Fine."

"I'd like to drop by and see him."

"Well, not tonight."

"What's happened, Charlie? Did he run away?"

"Yeh, but I'll find him."

He never did and thereafter when Charlie and I and a bunch of the guys got to talking about hunting and such and the subject of dog training came up, Charlie and I would tell the tale of Alfie.

"I bet I could have trained him," somebody would invariably say.

But Charlie and I knew otherwise, having learned the ultimate lesson: that once in a while you run across a dog that's just too good to do your bidding. And that's the one that gets away.

Jerome B. Robinson is a lifelong grouse hunter who lives in Lyme, New Hampshire, among the foothills of the White Mountains. He raises English setters and trains them in the grouse woods that straddle the New Hampshire-Vermont border. Robinson has been writing about bird dogs and bird hunting for the nation's leading outdoor magazines since 1967. He was gun dog editor at Sports Afield *for more than twenty years and is currently contributing editor and feature writer at* Field & Stream. *Robinson is the author of two gun dog training classics:* Hunt Close, *a guide to training pointing dogs for tight cover situations, and* Training the Hunting Retriever, *a step-by-step guide to training retrievers for real hunting situations.*

GUN DOG TRAINING

by Jerome Robinson

A glance through the sporting dog supply catalogs can give the mistaken impression that successful dog training relies upon varying degrees of punishment applied with whips, choke collars, pellet guns, and electronic shocking devices. So, before you become convinced that tools of punishment are necessary to dog training's everyday problems, let's make a few subtle observations.

The little old lady whose dog sits quietly beside her wherever she goes did not steady the dog with a sling shot, she probably just gave it a food tidbit whenever the dog sat quietly and withheld the treat when it did not.

Likewise, the old man whose dog delivers the newspaper to him each afternoon did not force-break the dog to retrieve by punishing it, he probably just rewarded the dog with a treat and a kind pat when it naturally copied him by picking up the newspaper and carrying it.

Given the opportunity, most dogs try to please the person who feeds them. They do this by copying that person; going where he goes, sitting when he sits, hunting if he hunts and bringing him whatever things he seems to like. Dogs do that without any so-called "training" at all if given the opportunity to learn what their masters like them to do.

Unfortunately, the idea that force and punishment are required to train sporting dogs has become widely accepted in spite of the fact that all other animals are primarily trained by rewarding them with food treats and affection when they behave as their trainers wish. So much emphasis has been placed on using sophisticated methods of force and punishment to train sporting dogs that training with food treats has been made to seem amateurish, yet logic tells us that the use of food treats should be the most effective means of getting a dog to do what you want.

Learning how to get food is any animal's strongest instinct. From the instant it draws its first breath an animal devotes its intellect to figuring out where food comes from and how to get it. Dogs are among the quickest animals to learn how to get food and are, therefore, among the easiest to train.

When a pup learns that it can win food treats by behaving in certain ways, it begins trying very hard to figure out which behaviors earn rewards and which do not. In no time you have a pupil that is not only willing, but eager, to comprehend what you want it to do.

There are no tricks to training with food rewards. Your job is simply to show the pup how to behave in certain ways and then to give each behavior a name that the dog can distinguish.

For instance, you can teach a pup to "sit" by holding a food treat (thin slices of hot dog make good treats—pups love them and always want more) over the pup's head. Move your hand back over the pup's head towards its tail. The pup will follow your hand with its nose and will fall backwards into a sitting position. The instant its fanny hits the floor, open your hand and let the pup have the treat.

Repeat the same maneuver three or four times, each time giving the pup the treat the instant it sits. Soon the pup will begin anticipating that it can win the treat by sitting and will

sit automatically when your treat-bearing hand appears. That's the behavior you want. Now give it a name. Say "sit" as you hold out the next treat and give the reward the instant the pup obeys.

In very short order the pup will learn what the word "sit" means and will be quick to respond to the command if you are always quick to reward it with a treat. Now begin encouraging it to sit for longer periods of time by withholding the treat. When the pup begins to stand up, repeat "sit" and reward the pup instantly when it obeys.

You can teach the pup to "lie down" by holding the hot dog treat in your closed fist and letting the pup smell it. Then drop your treat-bearing hand to the floor and move it slowly along the floor. The pup will follow your hand with its nose and will get down on its belly as you extend your hand away. The instant its belly hits the floor, open your hand and let the pup have the treat.

With a few repetitions the pup will automatically anticipate that lying down is another behavior that wins food rewards and will begin lying down as soon as your hand goes to the floor. That's the behavior you want, so give it a name. Say "lie down" next time you extend your hand and reward the pup the instant it complies.

Even a very young pup will learn to obey these simple commands quickly in order to win food rewards. You are appealing to its strongest instinct. The pup is learning how to make food happen.

Expand on the pup's eagerness to win a reward by gradually increasing the distance from which you give the command and by extending the time you make the pup continue the required behavior before you give the treat. Once it learns that compliance always wins a reward regardless of where you are when the command is given it will obey reliably. When it understands that it always gets the reward at the end, it will wait as you increase the length of time you require the command to stay in effect before the treat is given.

As you give the pup its treat at the end of each successful lesson, say "okay." This is a signal that the command it obeyed is no longer in effect and helps the pup to comprehend that it has completed the requirement of your command.

Already, you have a pup that has learned it can win food treats and your affection by obeying word commands. And you haven't punished it or forced it to do anything. Your pup likes you, trusts you and has no reason to fear you. Pups trained this way want to do things that please you.

You can easily teach a pup to "heel" by walking with it on a leash and holding the food treat at your knee. When the pup falls in beside you, say "heel" and give the reward at your knee as you proceed.

If you are consistent at restraining the pup with the leash when it pulls forward, using the leash to prevent it from dragging behind and giving it a food treat at your knee if it walks beside you when you say "heel", you will quickly have a pup that understands what "heel" means and knows what to do to get a food treat when it hears that command.

Teaching a pup to "come" on command is a cinch when food treats are used. When the pup has romped away from you for a short distance, get down on one knee, clap your hands to attract its attention and have a food treat ready to give when the pup bounds up to you.

Next time, don't bother clapping; just say "come" and the pup's name. Be sure to have the food treat ready. Practice at increasing distances and you will soon have a pup that is absolutely reliable at coming when called.

From the pup's point of view an interesting phenomenon is taking place. At an early age, without ever being punished or forced to do anything, the pup has formed a deeply rooted habit of obeying your commands. It knows how the system works. It has learned a few ways to win food rewards and please you at the same time and that knowledge gives the pup confidence and makes it want to learn more.

As the pup develops you can continue to build on that knowledge.

If you are wondering how you're going to keep a supply of hot dog slices on hand for all this treating, the answer is simple. Carry a sliced hot dog in a plastic sandwich bag in your pocket whenever you are with the pup and put the bag in the refrigerator when you're apart. The hot dogs will cost less than any tool of punishment and will enable you to train your pup to obey out of habit, not out of fear.

A pup that reliably comes, sits, lies down and heels on command, has learned the basics on which all degrees of higher training are founded. Once your pup responds reliably to those four basic commands, you can gradually replace hot dog treats with words of praise. Say "Good dog" and give the pup an affectionate pat each time it responds properly. Let your praise become the reward the dog earns by proper response and save the hot dog treats for teaching the proper responses to new lessons.

Well-bred sporting dogs come with certain special characteristics that have been established by many generations of selective breeding. You should not have to train a pointing dog to point, for instance, or a retriever to retrieve. Given the opportunity to rely on their own instincts, well-bred pointing dog pups will naturally hesitate before jumping in on a bird they smell but cannot see and well-bred retriever pups will pick things up and carry them without being trained to do so.

You will, however, need to train the pointing dog pup to hold its point for unnatural periods of time and the retriever will have to be trained to carry things straight back to you without fooling around and to deliver gently to your hand.

The easiest way to teach a dog to retrieve directly and gently to hand is, once again, to offer food treat rewards.

Most pups, regardless of breed, have some degree of natural retrieving instinct. If you toss a rolled up sock a few feet from a ten week old pup, it will probably run over and pick it up. Remain silent. Not knowing what to do next, the pup is very likely to run to you carrying the sock.

Have a hot dog slice ready and when the pup brings you the sock make a trade. Take hold of the sock and offer the hot dog slice simultaneously. The pup will automatically drop the sock in order to accept the treat and, presto, you have accomplished a completed retrieve and a gentle delivery to hand.

With repetition, the pup will get into the habit at a very early age of completing the retrieve quickly in order to win the reward and will relinquish the retrieved object instantly in trade for the hot dog slice. Two of retriever training's most troublesome tasks, the direct retrieve and a soft-mouthed delivery, will become a natural habit if you start a pup's retrieving training in this manner.

People usually don't send their dogs to professional trainers until the dogs are well grown, so the pros have had to develop training methods that apply to headstrong older dogs that probably have been allowed to develop habits that must be broken. That is why their training methods often depend on force and punishment.

As a puppy owner, however, you have a chance to start your pup off with good habits that make advanced training much easier for the dog to understand and force and punishment become unnecessary.

For example, there is no reason to wait for a pointing dog to grow up before putting it on birds. A well-bred pointing dog pup will point at eight to ten weeks of age if given the right introduction.

Here's how:

Dizzy a pigeon and place it in short grass with its head tucked under its wing, then lead your puppy up to the bird on leash. The pup will investigate the bird and probably will prod it with its nose or mouth it. When prodded the bird will flush and its flapping wings may startle the pup momentarily but within a moment the pup will settle down and want to sniff where the bird was.

Let it sniff. You are introducing it to the thrilling scent of birds.

Dizzy another pigeon and tuck it into short grass in the same place. This time bring the pup up on leash from the downwind side. When it smells the bird the pup may show excitement or it may show timidness. Say nothing and let Nature take its course.

Eventually, the pup will creep in close to the bird, using its nose. It may pounce on the bird or it may show a fear of touching it. Don't interfere, just watch. If the pup doesn't pounce on the bird and flush it, the bird will shortly wake up and flush on its own. Once the bird is gone, let the pup investigate where it was.

Now repeat the whole procedure one more time, planting a third dizzied pigeon in the same place, but this time hide the bird in the grass so that it cannot be seen from a distance. Again bring the pup up slowly from the downwind side.

Let the pup advance on slack leash at its own speed. This time, when the pup smells the bird but does not see it, it will freeze in hesitation knowing that the bird is close and not wanting to stumble into it. That hesitation is the foundation of the pointing instinct.

Let the pup stand there as long as it will. Imagine what the pup is experiencing. Bird scent is flooding its senses and the pup is awakening to the demands of its genetic instincts. At this tender age, you have introduced the pup to the thrill of bird scent and allowed its instincts to demand that it freeze and remain motionless.

As it stands on point, gently push the pup forward towards the bird. It will automatically resist being pushed into the bird and will stiffen back against your pressure and intensify its point. Stroke its tail up into a rigid position. Trail your fingers along its back from tail to head in a soothing gesture that assures the pup that its rigid attitude pleases you.

A pointing dog pup that is introduced to birds in this manner at eight to ten weeks of age forms a pointing habit before it is ever tempted to chase. With repetition of this lesson several times a week, you can develop a solid pointing dog that would rather point birds than flush and chase them.

If you follow this method and develop the pointing habit in a puppy before it is big enough to want to chase its birds, the rest of training becomes remarkably easy.

As the pup grows bigger, have it trail a short rope so that you can tie it to a bush or tree whenever it points. With the pup restrained, you can move past it to flush its bird and be assured that the pup cannot chase it. In this way you prevent the pup from ever having the chance to chase a bird that it pointed. A pup that points from instinct and lets you flush its birds without trying to chase forms a natural behavior pattern that avoids the need for force or punishment in training.

Controlling a gundog's hunting range in one of training's biggest headaches, particularly for those who buy pups from field trial stock which has been selectively bred for generations to run big. Nothing is harder than trying to keep a dog hunting close when its genes are goosing it to become a horizon-buster.

If you want a gundog that hunts at a pace suited to a man walking, buy a pup whose ancestors have been used successfully by hunters who hunt on their feet—it's as simple as that. With a dog that is bred to hunt at close to moderate range, you will be training in harmony with nature rather than against it.

When you have a pup that naturally wants to hunt near you, range control can be accomplished as a natural extension of the "come" command that you taught using food treats.

Once the pup is reliable at coming to you when you command "come," begin replacing the "come" command with a whistle signal. Call "come" followed by three beeps on your whistle. When the pup responds, slip it a food treat.

With a few repetitions, you can drop the verbal command and use the whistle signal alone, always rewarding the pup with a treat and an affectionate pat when it comes to you.

Use the whistle signal and a food treat to call the pup to you whenever it begins to range too far when hunting. Through repetition, show it that when it reaches a certain distance from you it is always called back. Eventually, the pup will recognize this distance and will begin to turn automatically when it gets out about that far.

From time to time, pause in your hunting and call the pup all the way to your side and give it a food treat when it comes up to you. Pat the pup. Take a break and have a moment of affection. Then send the pup ahead again and resume hunting. The pup will learn to look forward to these breaks and will be alert to where you are at all times. Its range will settle naturally into a comfortable pattern if you make it pleasant for the pup to be near you and reward it for responding correctly to your whistle signals.

All dogs respond eagerly to commands if they fully understand what they are being asked to do and have learned from experience that there is a desirable reward for responding correctly. Using food treats as bribes for correct responses is by far the most effective means of getting dogs to do things your way.

As you can see, food treats make it easy to teach the dog to come when it is called, sit and lie down on command, walk at heel, retrieve directly, deliver gently to hand and obey whistle signals with which you can control its hunting range. These methods are effective because they enable you to work with, rather than against, the dog's nature.

Encouraging bird dog pups to point before they are big enough to chase is effective for the same reason; you are working with the pup's raw basic instincts and teaching it behavior that pleases you before it discovers behavior that does not.

When dogs form desirable habits early, those habits are deeply ingrained and continue to influence how the dog will behave as it matures. If you continue to use logical training methods which are based upon reward for proper responses rather than punishment for incorrect responses, training will be fun for you and your dog and your days in the field together will be wonderfully satisfying.

Remember, a dog that fears your punishment learns to fear you. On the other hand, a dog that expects rewards tries hard to learn how to earn them and becomes intensely devoted to the person who shows it how to succeed.

This edition of *A Breed Apart, Volume II* was printed offset by Data Reproductions Corporation of Rochester Hills, Michigan. The book was designed by Angela Saxon of Saxon Design, Traverse City, Michigan. It is set in New Baskerville, a typeface created by British printer John Baskerville of Birmingham in about 1752. The Baskerville design has a delicacy and grace that come from long, elegant serifs and the subtle transfer of stroke weight from thick to very thin. The special limited edition of this book is bound in Cabra leather and available in a signed and numbered edition of 500 copies.